HARPERESSENTIALS

Want to play?

At the best parties, everything seems to be spontaneous and fun. Invariably, such gatherings have been carefully planned and prepared.

An essential ingredient for any party is a good selection of games. Choose the games you want to play well in advance, and make sure that you have the equipment you need. It is important to select a good mix, keeping in mind the ages and personalities of your guests.

With a little thought and planning, games can help to provide amusement for all concerned, and offer a welcome break during the proceedings.

Other HarperEssentials

Family
And Party
Games

Trevor Bounford and
The Diagram Group

HarperTorch
An Imprint of HarperCollins*Publishers*

This book was originally published in 2001 by HarperCollins UK.

❦
HARPERTORCH
An Imprint of HarperCollins*Publishers*
10 East 53rd Street
New York, New York 10022-5299

First HarperTorch paperback printing: December 2003

10 9 8 7 6 5 4 3 2 1

INTRODUCTION

An essential ingredient for any family get-together, or party, is a good selection of games to play. With a little thought and planning, games can help to provide amusement for all concerned, and provide a welcome break during the proceedings.

HarperEssentials Family and Party Games is a fascinating, highly illustrated guide to almost 150 games and activities, most of which can be played by children over the age of five, and by adults of any age. Each game details the minimum age group, the optimum number of players, the aim of the game, any preparation required, and the various stages in the game itself. With each activity there are step-by-step instructions and clear, accurate diagrams showing techniques and methods that are easy to follow. The games are arranged under specific categories, such as action, musical, racing, dice or spoken word games, and include old favorites such as Hide and Seek, Pin the Tail on the Donkey, and Tongue-twisters, as well as newer activities such as Aggression, Botticelli and Telegrams. Additionally, to make finding the right game easy, this book includes indexes of games by appropriate age and games defined by a certain number of players, plus sections on organizing games and useful equipment.

HarperEssentials Family and Party Games is an attractive companion volume to *Card Games*.

CONTENTS

Musical Games

Picture Games

Racing Games

Dice Games

Pick Up Sticks

GAMES BY AGE

Games for age 3+

Games for age 5+

Games for ages 5–10

Games for age 7+

Games for age 8+

Games for age 9+

Games for age 10+

GAMES BY PLAYERS

Games for 2 players

Games for groups of players

Games for teams of players

ADVICE FOR GIVING A PARTY

At the best parties everything seems to be spontaneous and fun. Invariably, such parties have been carefully planned and prepared.

As a general rule, the younger the party-goers, the less planning you have to do. Very young children up to five years old don't need much more than a few simple games to keep them happy. Five to 10-year-olds are more demanding and will expect a variety of games and activities. For the over-10s you will need to choose games and activities imaginatively. Young people are often self-conscious and easily embarrassed.

Choose the games you want to play well in advance, and make sure that you have the equipment you need for each game. It is important to select a good mix of games, bearing in mind the ages and characters of your guests. Try to avoid playing too many active games one after the other—mix active games with quiet games or quizzes to give the guests a chance to recuperate.

Prepare more games than you think you will need, and have a good supply of prizes. If you are planning some outdoor games, remember to prepare extra indoor games in case the weather is against you. Many games, such as Musical Bumps, need to have someone in charge to control the music and settle disputes. And games involving rough and tumble may need supervision to stop them from getting out of hand.

Handy rules

❀ Give clear instructions to everyone before each game.

❀ Don't let any one game go on too long.

❀ Have plenty of space if players need to move about.

❀ Consolation prizes for losers are often a good idea.

❀ Boisterous games are best played before any meal.

USEFUL EQUIPMENT

The equipment required is specified at the beginning of each game. Some of the games require specific equipment, such as dice, pick up sticks or tiddlywinks, but most of the other things you will need can be found around the house. Each category of game uses similar equipment, but in general the following will be handy.

✿ A scarf to serve as a blindfold.
✿ Pencils (one for each player with a few in reserve) and plenty of paper.
✿ Wrapping paper, blank postcards.
✿ A cassette player or musical instruments.
✿ A selection of different-sized balls.
✿ String and rope.
✿ Plenty of balloons are essential for any children's party, and some of the games make use of them.

Action
Games

MY LiTTLE BiRD

Age 3+
Players Group

This
game is
played in
countries
all over the
world. Other
names for it
include Flying
High and Birds
Fly.

Play

❀ One player is the
   leader and the others stand
   in a row in front of him. Alternatively, everyone sits around a table.

❀ The leader starts by saying "My little
   bird is lively, is lively," and then goes on to
   name something followed by the word "fly"—for
   example, he might say "eggs fly."

❀ If whatever he names can fly—for example,
   cockatoos—the players raise their arms and
   wave them about. If it cannot fly—as with
   eggs—the players should remain still.

❀ A player who makes a mistake is out. The last
   player left in the game wins.

DEAD LIONS

Age 3+   **Players Group**

Aim
The player staying still the longest is the winning dead lion.

Preparation
The organizer gets all the players to lie motionless on the ground or floor.

Play
✿ The organizer disqualifies every player who moves until only one dead lion is left lying. This last player is the winner. All disqualified players try to make the others move without actually touching them.

CHARADES

Age 7+
Players Teams

Charades is probably the best-known and most popular of all games involving acting.

Aim
For one team to guess a word with several syllables, or the title of a book or film, that is acted out in mime by another team.

Equipment
Some dressing-up clothes will add to the fun but are not absolutely necessary.

Book   **Film**

Preparation

It is probably a good idea to prepare some good subjects beforehand if children are involved. Good examples include words such as Bandage, Carpet, Earring and Knapsack, or film and book titles.

Television

Play

❀ The first team chooses its title or word and indicates the type of subject using one of the set mimes shown here.

Play/theater

Song/musical

The team then indicates how many words and syllables the title contains by holding up fingers. It then acts out each word or syllable separately, or the whole word or title together. There are several ways of giving clues, such as indicating a short word, the word "the," the word of the title sounds like the one being mimed.

* ❋ The second team tries to guess what the word or title is.
* ❋ The game is played in turn by the teams, with the team with most correct guesses the winner.

Sounds like

Number of words

Number of syllables

Small word

"The"

HIDE AND SEEK

Age 7+   *Players* **Group**

One of the best-loved and most enduring of all children's games.

Aim
To get "home" without being touched.

Play
* One player is made "seeker" and covers his or her eyes and counts to 40 while the others go and hide.
* The seeker then has to try to find players and touch them.
* The players must try to reach home without being touched—better still, without being seen by the seeker. The players who are caught are out.
* The last player to be caught is the winner and can take the place of the seeker.

HUNT THE THIMBLE

Age 5+   **Players** Group

This very popular game is usually played with a thimble, but any other small object will do just as well.

Play

❀ All the players but one leave the room while the player left behind hides the thimble somewhere in the room or on his or her person. He then calls the other players back into the room to look for it.

❀ The game is won by the first player to find the thimble and take it to the player who hid it. The finder then has a turn at hiding the thimble.

TREASURE HUNT

Age 5+   **Players Group**

Preparation

Considerable preparation is required because the host has to write a story about buried treasure. The story should not be too long and should contain a number of clues as to where the treasure can be found. For example, a reference in the story to the beach could be a clue to a sandpit in the garden. The "treasure" may be any item and may be hidden indoors or out.

Play

* Players are given a copy of the story, or the host reads it out to them. The players then set off to search for the treasure. They must not talk to each other during the hunt. A time limit of, say, 15 minutes should be allowed.
* The winner is the first player to find the treasure, which may double as a prize.

IN THE MANNER OF THE WORD

Age 9+   ***Players*** **Group**

This is an amusing act-
ing game in which play-
ers attempt to guess
adverbs.

Play

❋ One player
chooses an
adverb, such as
rapidly, quietly or
amusingly. The other
players in turn then
ask him to carry out
some action "in the
manner of the word."
For example, a player
might say, "Eat in the
manner of the word,"
"Walk in the manner of
the word," or "Laugh in
the manner of the
word."

❋ The player who chooses the adverb
must do as the other players ask, and the other
players may make guesses as soon as acting
begins.

❋ The first player to guess an adverb correctly scores one point. If no one guesses the word after each of the players has asked for an action, the player who chose the adverb receives one point.

❋ The game is won by the player with most points after each of the players has had a turn at choosing the adverb.

MATCHING PAIRS

Ages 5-10   ***Players* Group**

Equipment
A number of everyday articles are needed and some wrapping paper.

Preparation
The host thinks of a "pair" of items for each of the guests. Examples might include: salt and pepper, knife and fork, sock and shoe, a pair of gloves, a cup and saucer, a King and Queen (from a set of playing cards). The host wraps up one part of each "pair" and hides the other somewhere in the room.

Play
✿ Players are given a part of their "pair."
✿ They have to look for what they think is likely to be the other, which has been hidden by the host.
✿ Every player who matches his pair within ten minutes or so is a winner.

SARDINES

Age 7+   **Players Group**

This is a type of Hide and Seek (see page 8) usually played in the dark. The more rooms that can be played in the more exciting the game becomes.

Aim

To find and join the "sardine."

Play

* One player is chosen as "sardine" to go and hide (preferably somewhere big enough for most of the others to squeeze in, too) while all the others cover their eyes and count to 30.

* The seekers then go off individually to find the sardine.

* When a seeker locates the sardine, he or she joins the sardine in the hiding place. Eventually the hiding place is full of hiders, while fewer and fewer seekers remain.

* There are no winners in this game. The last player to find the hiding place becomes the next sardine.

SIMON SAYS

Age **3+**
Players **Group**

This is an old party
game that remains a
great favorite.

Play

✿ One player is the
  leader and the others
  spread around the
  room in front of him
  or her.
✿ The leader orders the others to
  make various actions—such as
  touching their toes or raising
  their arms. Whether or not they must
  obey the orders depends on how the
  orders are given.
✿ If the leader begins the order with the words
  "Simon says," the players must obey. If he does
  not begin with these words, they must not make
  the action. If a player makes a mistake, he or she
  is out of the game. The leader can encourage
  mistakes by giving rapid orders; by developing a
  rhythm with a repeated pattern of movements
  and then breaking it; or by making the actions
  himself for the others to follow.
✿ The last person left in the game is the winner
  and becomes the next leader.

TRIANGULAR TUG-OF-WAR

Age 10+   **Players** Group

Equipment
A 6–9 ft (2–3 m) length of rope (or cord) and three handkerchiefs are required.

Preparation
Tie the ends of the rope together. If indoors, make sure you have a large area clear of furniture. Get three players to stand outside the rope and hold it with one hand behind them to form a triangle. Place a handkerchief on the ground in front of each player.

Play

✸ The players have to hold on to the rope behind them and pick up the handkerchief in front of them. Each should be aware of his opponents though, and pull the rope to make sure they don't get to their handkerchiefs first.

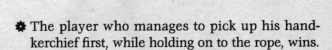

✸ The player who manages to pick up his handkerchief first, while holding on to the rope, wins.

WHAT'S THE TIME, MR. WOLF?

Age 5+
Players Group

Preparation
One player chooses to be or is chosen as Mr. Wolf.

Play
❀ Mr. Wolf stands with his back to the others, who advance one step at a time toward him from a reasonable distance. At each step, one member of the advancing group shouts, "What's the time, Mr. Wolf?"

❀ The time is given by him, and the group takes another step forward.

❀ At a moment of his own choosing Mr. Wolf will, instead, shout the reply, "Dinner Time!" He then turns rapidly and chases the others. The player who's caught becomes Mr. Wolf.

Ball
Games

BROKEN BOTTLES

Age 10+   **Players Group**

Equipment
A softball is
needed.

Play
❋ Players form a
circle and
throw the ball
to each other,
catching with
both hands.

❋ When a player
drops or misses
the ball, he or
she pays a
penalty. The first
penalty is to use
only the right
hand. The sec-
ond is to use
only the left.
The third is to
have one knee

on the floor, but use both hands, the fourth, to
be on both knees. The fifth, to be on both knees
and use only the right hand, and lastly, sixth, to
be on both knees and to use only the left hand.
After that, the player drops out.

❀ The player who survives longest wins.

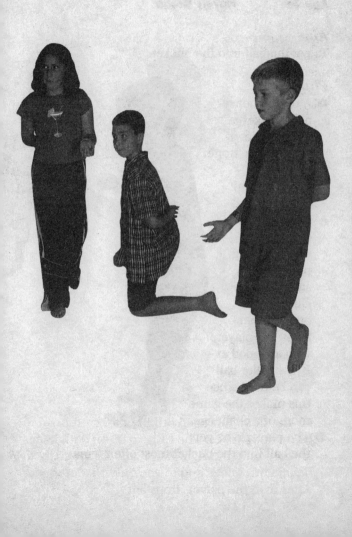

BUCKET BALL

Age 3+   **Players Group**

Aim
To get the ball into the bucket.

Play
* A plastic house-
  hold bucket is
  weighed down
  with a large stone
  or brick.
* Players stand
  around it and
  take turns to
  throw a ball
  into it. Young
  players can
  stand fairly
  close, older
  ones further
  back. For players
  who are good at
  it, a smaller ball
  can be used since
  this makes the game
  more of a challenge.
* The player who gets
  the ball into the bucket most often wins.

CIRCLE BALL

Ages 5–10   **Players** Group

This game is best played on a hard surface. It is a fast and energetic game played only for enjoyment.

Aim
Players bounce a ball to each other in turn.

Play

❋ A circle about 3 ft (1 m) across is drawn, and players form a circle around it, standing several feet back.

❋ A ball is thrown from player to player in order, and must bounce inside the drawn circle. Players must catch it before it bounces again.

GUARD THE GATE

Ages 5–10   ***Players* Group**

Aim
To roll a ball through the "gate" formed by the space between players.

Play
❋ Players form a circle, each being one arm's length away from the next. The gate is the space to his or her right.

❋ The ball (a tennis ball would be suitable, or a larger ball for younger players) is rolled by hand by the players, each trying to send it through any of the spaces between players—the gates. At the same time the players must guard their own gates to stop the ball going through. Players who let the ball through their gates drop out.

❋ The player who succeeds in defending his or her gate the longest wins.

HOT POTATO

Ages 5-10   **Players** Group

Aim
For the players to keep the ball away from the player in the middle.

Play
✿ The players form a circle and one is chosen to stand in the center.

❉ The ball is thrown from player to player, and the one in the middle tries to intercept. He or she may win the ball by touching it at any time, even if one of the other players is holding it, or it falls outside the circle. Whoever makes the mistake that allows the player in the middle to touch the ball takes his or her place.

❉ The game goes on until all the players have a turn in the middle. The one who holds out longest may be declared the winner.

WALL GAME

Age 5+   *Players* **Group**

Aim
To throw and catch a ball quickly.

Play
❀ Each player is given a number. They stand near the wall in no particular order.

❀ The first player starts the game by throwing the ball against the wall, at the same time calling the number of one of the other players.

❀ That player has to try to catch the ball after the first bounce.

❀ If the player succeeds, he or she throws the ball and calls another number.

❀ If he or she fails, the first player throws again and calls a different number.

❀ The game can be scored, with points given for every successful catch. The highest score within a time limit wins.

Blindfold
Games

BLIND MAN'S BLUFF

Age 7+   **Players** Group

Aim
A blindfolded player tries to catch and identify another player.

Play
❀ A blind person is chosen and blindfolded. He or she is turned around three times in the center of the room and then left alone.

❀ The other players dance around, taunting the blindfolded person and dodging out of his or her way to avoid capture.

❀ When the blindfolded person catches someone, he or she has two or three guesses at the name of the prisoner. If he guesses correctly, the prisoner becomes the new blind man. If wrong, he continues to be the blind man and tries to catch another player.

BLIND JUDGMENT

Age 7+   **Players** Group

Play
❀ One player is blindfolded and placed on a "seat of judgment."

❀ Another player then stands quietly in front of him, and the player in the judgment seat gives a brief description of whoever he thinks might be standing in front of him.

- If the other players think that the "blind judgment" was reasonably accurate, the player in front of the blindfolded player becomes the new blind man.
- If his judgment was inaccurate, the original blind man must pass judgment on another player.

THIEVES

Age 7+   **Players Group**

Aim

A blindfolded player tries to catch players stealing from him or her.

Play

- One player is blindfolded and given a rolled paper or other soft implement to hold in his or her hand.
- The blindfolded player sits in the middle of a circle made by the other players, and a pile of treasure—necklaces, brooches, bracelets, etc.—is placed in front of him or her.
- Players in the circle quietly take it in turns to steal a piece of treasure. If the blindfolded person hears a thief, he or she strikes at him or her with the newspaper and calls "thief, thief."
- If he or she touches a thief, the thief must return empty-handed to his or her place to await the next turn.
- The thief who collects most treasure wins the game.

BLIND MAN'S TREASURE HUNT

Age 7+   **Players** Group

Equipment

Parcels of different sizes and shapes, at least one for each player, plus several extra to allow choice for all players, and a blindfold, are needed.

Preparation

All the players must be sent out of the room. The parcels are then placed on a table in the middle of the room.

Play

✿ Bring in the guests one by one, blindfolded.

✿ Lead them up to the table and tell them they may choose one present, but must not open it until everyone has chosen.

✿ Everyone "wins" something in this game. The fun lies in the opening of the presents, and guessing what they are from their shape and sound.

PIN THE TAIL ON THE DONKEY

Age 5+   **Players Group**

Aim
Blindfolded players try to pin a tail in the correct position on a drawing of a tail-less donkey.

Preparation
The organizer draws a large picture of a donkey without a tail and fastens it onto a pinboard propped upright. He also makes a donkey's tail out of cardboard or wool and sticks a large pin through the body end.

Play
❀ Each player in turn is blindfolded and turned around so that he is in front of and facing the donkey. He is then given the tail and attempts to pin it on the correct part of the donkey.

✻ The organizer marks the position of each player's attempt.

✻ The player who pins nearest the correct place is the winner.

Contest
Games

AGGRESSION

Age 9+   **Players 2**

Aim
Players fight imaginary battles and try to occupy the maximum amount of territory.

Equipment
Each player must have a crayon of a different color.

Playing area
A large sheet of paper is used. One player begins by drawing the boundaries of an imaginary country; the other player then draws the outline of another imaginary country. Any agreed number of countries may be drawn (20 is an average number), and they can be any shape or size. When the agreed number of countries has been drawn, each is clearly marked with a different letter of the alphabet.

Armies
Each player is allotted 100 armies. Taking turns, each chooses a country (who drew the boundary has no bearing on the choice) that he or she intends to occupy and writes within it how many armies he or she is allocating to it. (Once a country has been occupied, no player may add further armies to it.) This procedure continues until all the countries have been occupied or until each player has allocated all his or her armies.

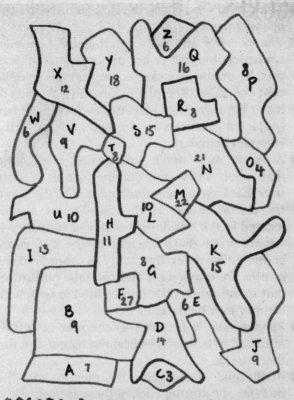

Green: used 100 armies, won 6 countries.

Blue: used 100 armies, won 9 countries.

Red: used 91 armies, won 11 countries

Play

- ❋ The player who chose the first country has the opening move.
- ❋ The player's aim is to retain more occupied countries than his or her opponent; to achieve this, he or she "attacks" enemy armies in adjacent countries. The player announces which of his or her territories will attack which neighbor. (Adjacent countries are defined as those with a common boundary.)
- ❋ A player may attack with armies from more than one country, provided they are all in countries that have a common border with the country under attack. If the number of armies located in the attacking country or countries is greater than those located in the defending country, the defending army is conquered; its armies are crossed off and can take no further part in the game. (The armies used to conquer a country may be reused.)
- ❋ Players take it in turns to conquer countries until one or both of them cannot mount any further attacks.
- ❋ At the end of the game the players total the number of countries each of them retains.
- ❋ The winner is the player with the highest number of unconquered countries—he or she need not necessarily be the player who made the greatest number of conquests.

APPLE BOBBING

Age 5+   **Players Group**

Equipment
A large bowl, lots of apples, newspapers (in case of spillage) and a towel are needed.

Preparation
Fill the bowl with water, place it on newspapers and put a number of apples into the water.

Play
✿ Players take turns in trying to retrieve an apple from the bowl, using only their mouths.

✿ There are no real winners, since everybody should end up with an apple. Perhaps a small prize could be given to the player who gets his or her apple in the shortest time.

APPLE ON A STRING

Age 7+   **Players** Group

This game is an old favorite for Halloween. Players try, without using their hands, to eat apples suspended from strings.

Play

❀ A piece of string is hung across the room, well above head height. An apple (or doughnut) per person is suspended from it, also on a string.

❀ The players try to eat their apples or doughnuts without using their hands.

❀ The first player to eat the apple down to its core, or to finish eating the doughnut, is the winner.

ARM WRESTLING

Age 7+   *Players 2*

Play

✤ Two players sit facing each other at either side of a table. Resting their right elbows on the table so that the elbows touch and with crooked arms, they clasp each other's right hands. (Both players may use their left arms if they prefer.)

✤ On the signal to begin, each player tries to force his opponent's right hand back until it touches the table. Elbows must be kept firmly on the table.

✤ The winner is the first to succeed.

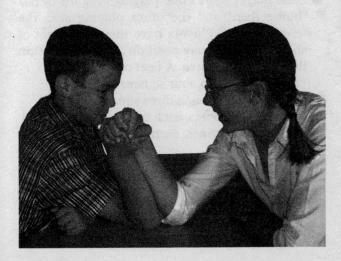

BATTLESHIPS

Age 10+   **Players 2**

Aim

The objective is to destroy an opponent's entire fleet by a series of "hits."

Play

❋ The players should sit so that they cannot see each other's papers. Each of them draws two identical playing areas, 10 squares by 10 squares in size. In order to identify each square, the playing areas have numbers down one side and letters across the top (thus the top left-hand square is A1; the bottom left-hand square is A10, etc.).

❋ Each player marks one playing area his or her "home fleet" and the other playing area the "enemy fleet." Players have their own fleet of ships that they may position anywhere within their home fleet area. A fleet comprises:
  a) one battleship, four squares long;
  b) two cruisers, each three squares long;
  c) three destroyers, each two squares long; and
  d) four submarines, each one square only.

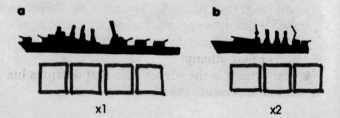

a   b

x1   x2

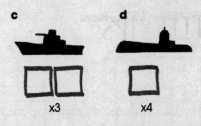

● Players "position" their ships by outlining the appropriate number of squares. The squares representing each ship must be in a row or column (see page 50). There must also be at least one vacant square between ships. Players take turns.

● In each turn, a player may attempt three hits: he or she calls out the names of any three squares, marking them on the enemy fleet area as he or she does so.

● The player's opponent must then consult his or her own home fleet area to see whether any of these squares are occupied.

● If they are, he or she must state how many and the category of ship hit. In order to sink a ship, every one of its component squares must receive a hit.

● The game continues with both players marking the state of their own and the enemy's fleet— this may be done by shading or outlining squares, or in some other manner (see page 51). There is no limit to the number of hits each player may attempt.

● The winner is the player who first destroys his or her opponent's fleet.

Battleships: Player 1's positions

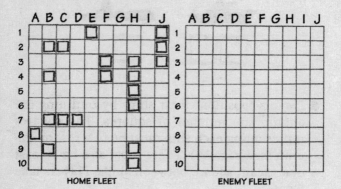

HOME FLEET   ENEMY FLEET

Battleships: Player 2's positions

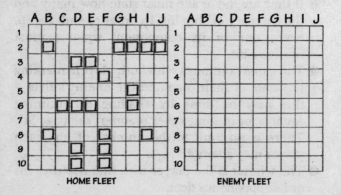

HOME FLEET   ENEMY FLEET

Game in progress: Player 1

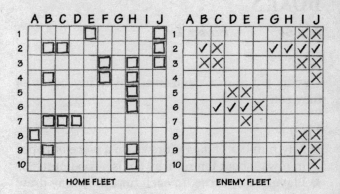

HOME FLEET   ENEMY FLEET

Game in progress: Player 2

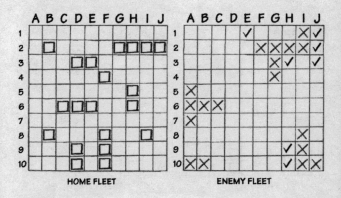

HOME FLEET   ENEMY FLEET

BOXES

Age 5+   **Players 2**

Aim
Players try to draw and initial as many boxes as they can.

Play
❋ Any number of dots is drawn on a piece of paper in rows. About ten rows by ten is a good number.

❋ Players take turns. In each turn they may draw a horizontal or vertical line to join up any two dots that are next to each other.

❋ Whenever a player completes a box, he or she initials it and may then draw another line that does not complete a box.

❋ As soon as there are no more dots to be joined— all the boxes having been completed—the game ends.

Example of grid

Game in progress

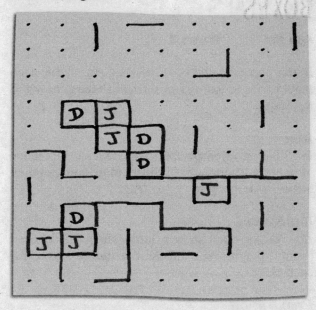

Winning
The player with the highest number of initialed boxes is the winner.

Variation
Another way of playing is to try to form as few boxes as possible—the players join up as many dots as they can before being forced to complete a box. The winner is the player with the lowest number of initialed boxes.

CRYSTALS

Age 10+   *Players 2*

In this sophisticated pattern-visualizing game, each player tries to form symmetrical shapes known as "crystals."

Aim

Each player attempts to "grow" crystals on a piece of paper with the aim of filling more squares than his or her opponent.

Equipment

All that is needed is a large sheet of squared (graph) paper and a differently colored crayon for each player.

Preparation

A grid of 20 rows of 20 squares each would form a suitable area. A player does not score points for the number of crystals he or she grows, but for the number of squares covered by the crystals he or she claims.

A crystal is made up of "atoms," each of which occupies a single square. Atoms are added by either of the players until the crystal is completed.

In growing crystals, players must observe certain rules of symmetry that determine whether or not a crystal is legitimate. The symmetry of a crystal can be determined by visualizing four axes through its center: horizontal, vertical and two diagonal axes.

Once the axes have been "drawn," it should theoret-
ically be possible to fold the crystal along each of
the four axes to produce corresponding "mirror"
halves that, when folded, exactly overlay each other
(i.e. are the same shape and size).

Crystals: rules for building

✓ = legitimate crystals   ✗ = not legitimate

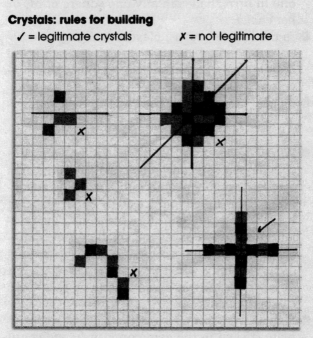

In addition to the rules of symmetry, players must
observe the following:

    a) a legitimate crystal may be formed from four
       or more atoms drawn by one player only;

    b) the atoms forming a crystal must be joined
       along their sides—they may not be con-
       nected only by their corners;

    c) a crystal may not contain any empty atoms (i.e. holes).

Play

✿ Players decide on their playing order, and each one in turn shades in any one square of his or her choice.

✿ In the first few turns, players rarely try to grow crystals. Instead, they place single atoms around the playing area in order to establish potential crystal sites.

✿ As play progresses, players will see which atoms are best placed for growing crystals and add to them as appropriate.

✿ When a player thinks he or she has grown a crystal, he or she declares it, and rings the area that it covers. A player with a winning advantage will try to retain the lead by either blocking his or her opponents' attempts at growing crystals, or by growing several small crystals that— although not high scoring—restrict the playing area. Play ends when no blank squares are left or when the players agree that no more crystals can be formed.

✿ Players work out which of the crystals are legitimate (ticked in the game opposite), and count the number of squares each covers. Any crystal that does not demonstrate symmetry around each of the four axes is not legitimate and does not score.

✿ The number of squares in the legitimate crystals that each player has grown is added up, and the player with most squares wins the game.

Crystals: examples

✓ = legitimate crystals   ✗ = not legitimate

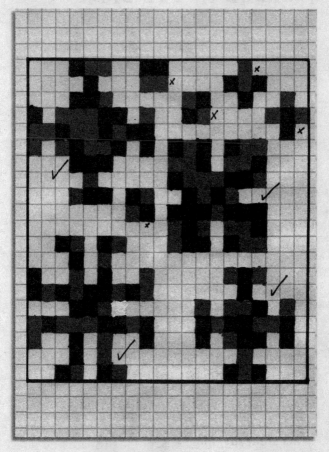

MURDER IN THE DARK

Age 10+ **Players** Group

Equipment
Envelopes, paper and a pen.

Preparation
One person must hand out sealed envelopes to the players. Only two of them have anything written on the piece of paper inside. On one is written "You are the murderer." The other says "You are the detective."

Play
❋ The players open their envelopes, and the player who has been chosen to play the "detective" lets everyone know of this. (The others must keep quiet about the contents of their envelopes, of course.)

❋ When all the players are ready, the detective turns out the lights for one minute.

- During this time, the players mill about in the dark and the "murderer" commits the crime by *very gently* squeezing someone's neck.
- The moment the victim feels the murderer's hands, he or she must scream loudly and fall to the floor.
- Meanwhile, the "murderer" must try to get as far away from the scene of the crime as possible in order to appear innocent.
- A few seconds after the scream, the detective puts the lights back on, noting the positions of all the players.
- The detective asks the players questions about the "murder." They must all answer truthfully, except the murderer, who may lie as much as he or she likes.
  - When the detective thinks he or she has deduced the identity of the murderer, he officially accuses someone.
  - If the detective is correct, the murderer must confess. But if he is wrong (and he only gets one guess), the murderer wins and the mystery remains unsolved.

ROCK, PAPER, SCISSORS

Age 10+   **Players 2**

This ancient game, also known as Hic, Haec, Hoc and by many other names, is played all over the world. Three objects (rock, a piece of paper, and scissors) are indicated by different positions of the hand:

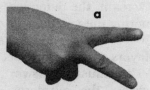

a) two fingers making a V shape represent scissors;
b) an open hand represents a piece of paper; and
c) a clenched fist represents a rock.

Aim

To guess correctly and to win the maximum number of rounds.

Play

 Two players hide one hand behind their backs and adopt one of the three positions.

 One player calls "One, two, three" (or "Hic, haec, hoc") and as the third number or word is called the players show their hands.

 The winner of a round is decided with reference

to the following statements: scissors can cut paper; paper may be wrapped around a rock; and a rock can blunt the scissors. Thus, if one player chooses scissors and the other player paper, the player who chooses scissors wins the round. If both players decide on the same object, the round is a draw. Players usually play a predetermined number of rounds.

✱ The winner is the player who wins the largest number of rounds.

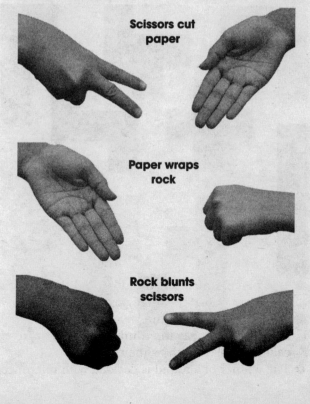

Scissors cut paper

Paper wraps rock

Rock blunts scissors

SHAPING UP

Age 10+   **Players 2**

Equipment
In advance, prepare the shapes shown here from card. There should be one whole set per player. Note that each shape comprises five squares.

Play

✿ Players are asked to make up different shapes and are given a time limit, perhaps 4 or 5 minutes, for each. Examples might include a rectangle that is 5 by 12 squares, 3 by 20 squares, and so on.

✿ Each square used scores one point. For example, a rectangle of 5 by 12 squares would score 60 points.

✿ After, say, six test challenges, the player with the most points is declared the winner.

45 points

25 points

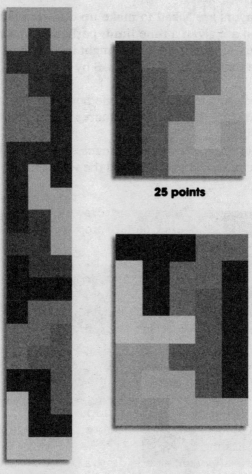

25 points

60 points

35 points

SPROUTS

Ages 5-10   ***Players 2***

Sprouts has certain similarities with Boxes, but needs rather more ingenuity to win!

Aim
The players try to be the last to complete a "sprout" within the allowed moves.

Play
❀ About six or so dots are drawn—well spaced out—on a sheet of paper (more may be drawn for a longer game).

❀ Taking turns, each player draws a line joining any two dots or joining a dot to itself.

❀ This player then draws a dot anywhere along the line he or she has just made, and his or her turn ends. When drawing a line, the following rules must be observed:
  a) no line may cross itself;
  b) no line may cross a line that has already been drawn;
  c) no line may be drawn through a dot;
  d) a dot may have no more than three lines leaving it.

❀ The last person able to draw a legitimate line is the winner.

Sprouts: foul lines

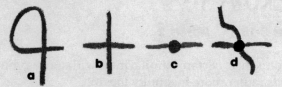

a   b   c   d

Sprouts: a sample game

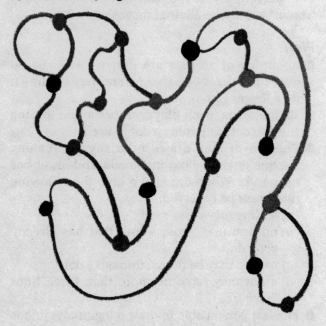

TIC-TAC-TOE

Age 5+   **Players 2**

Aim
To place three adjoining marks on a grid.

Play
❋ Two vertical lines are drawn with two horizontal lines crossing them, forming nine spaces. Players decide which of them is to draw O's (circles) and which of them X's.

❋ Taking turns, players make their mark in any vacant space.

❋ The winner is the player who manages to get three of his or her marks in a row (horizontally, vertically or diagonally). He or she then draws a line through his or her winning row and the game comes to an end. If neither player succeeds in forming a row, the game is considered drawn. As the player who draws first has a better chance of winning, players usually swap their starting order after each game.

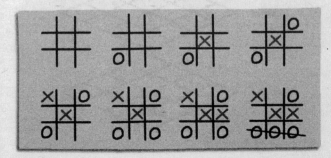

THREE-DIMENSIONAL TIC-TAC-TOE

Age 10+   **Players 2**

Based on the standard game, the three-dimensional version offers a lengthier and more challenging alternative. It can be bought as a game but can equally well be played with pencil and paper.

Three-dimensional Tic-tac-toe

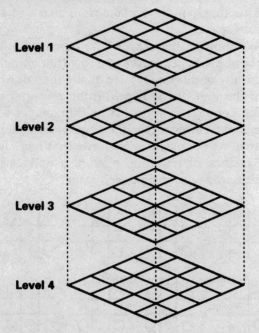

Level 1

Level 2

Level 3

Level 4

Aim

Players aim to complete a line of their marks in any of the three dimensions.

Play

✿ The cube may be represented diagrammatically by 64 squares—as shown opposite. For actual play, each "layer" of the cube is drawn out individually.

✿ Play then proceeds as in Tic-tac-toe.

✿ The winner is the first player to get four of his or her marks in a row (illustrations overleaf show winning rows).

Horizontal win

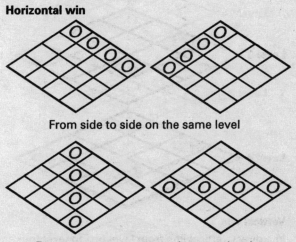

From side to side on the same level

From corner to corner on the same level

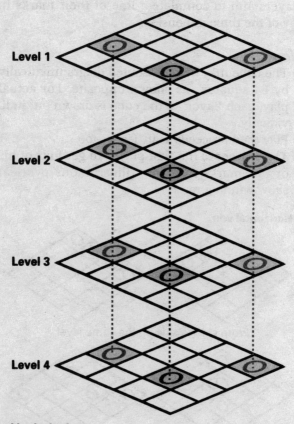

Level 1

Level 2

Level 3

Level 4

Vertical win

In a direct vertical line from level one to level four.

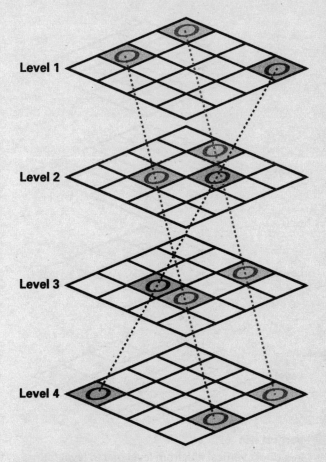

Vertical diagonal win

In a direct diagonal line from level one to level four.

Musical
Games

HERE WE GO ROUND THE MULBERRY BUSH

Age 3+   **Players Group**

Play

❀ The players form a circle and hold hands.

❀ During the first verse, they dance around in a circle.

❀ For each of the subsequent verses they perform the actions described and then join hands again for the chorus.

Chorus
Here we go round the mulberry bush,
the mulberry bush, the mulberry bush,
Here we go round the mulberry bush,
So early in the morning.

1
This is the way we wash our face, wash our face, wash
our face,
This is the way we wash our face
So early in the morning.

2
This is the way we brush our teeth, brush our teeth,
brush our teeth,
This is the way we brush our teeth,
So early in the morning.

3
This is the way we comb our hair, comb our hair, comb
our hair,
This is the way we comb our hair,
So early in the morning.

4
This is the way we walk to school, walk to school, walk
to school,
This is the way we walk to school,
So early in the morning.

5
This is the way we run home from school, run home
from school, run home from school,
This is the way we run home from school,
So early in the morning.

LONDON BRIDGE

Age 3+   **Players** Group

Preparation

Two players are chosen to be the bridge. Each chooses to be either silver or gold.

Play

❀ The bridge is formed by the two players joining hands.

❀ The rest dance in a circle, passing under the bridge. On the word "lady" the arms of the bridge come down and catch one of the dancers.

❀ They ask, "What will you pay me, silver or gold?" Depending on the answer, the captured player stands behind one side of the bridge and

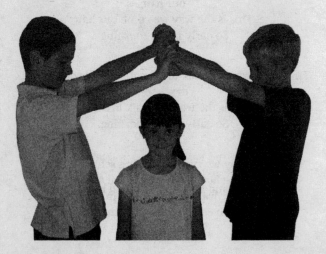

the game goes on until all the dancers are
caught. Often, the game ends with the two lines
of players having a tug-of-war.

London Bridge is falling down, falling down, falling down,
London Bridge is falling down,
My fair lady.

Build it up with sticks and stones,
sticks and stones, sticks and stones,
Build it up with sticks and stones,
My fair lady.

Sticks and stones will fall away, fall away, fall away,
Sticks and stones will fall away,
My fair lady.

Build it up with iron bars, iron bars, iron bars,
Build it up with iron bars,
My fair lady.

Irons bars will bend and break,
bend and break, bend and break,
Iron bars will bend and break,
My fair lady.

Build it up with pins and nails,
pins and nails, pins and nails,
Build it up with pins and nails,
My fair lady.

Pins and nails will rust and break,
rust and break, rust and break,
Pins and nails will rust and break,
My fair lady.

OLD MACDONALD HAD A FARM

Age **3+**   *Players* **Group**

Play

❀ The players form a circle, standing or sitting.

❀ As each verse is sung, they imitate the animal sounds, and repeat all the other noises of the previous verses, so that as the game proceeds it becomes very raucous and exciting. The game can be extended for several more verses to include, for instance, cats, pigs, frogs, horses, and so on.

Old MacDonald had a farm, ee-aye-ee-aye-o,
And on that farm he had some cows, ee-aye-ee-aye-o,
With a Moo-moo here, and a Moo-moo there,
Here a Moo, there a Moo, everywhere a Moo-moo,
Old MacDonald had a farm, ee-aye-ee-aye-o.

Old MacDonald had a farm, ee-aye-ee-aye-o,
And on that farm he had some ducks, ee-aye-ee-aye-o,
With a Quack-quack here, and a Quack-quack there,
Here a Quack, there a Quack, everywhere a Quack-quack,
With a Moo-moo here, and a Moo-moo there,
Here a Moo, there a Moo, everywhere a Moo-moo,
Old MacDonald had a farm, ee-aye-ee-aye-o.

Old MacDonald had a farm, ee-aye-ee-aye-o,
And on that farm he had some sheep, ee-aye-ee-aye-o,
With a Baa-baa here, and a Baa-baa there,
Here a Baa, there a Baa, everywhere a Baa-baa,
With a Quack-quack here, and a Quack-quack there,
Here a Quack, there a Quack, everywhere a Quack-quack,
With a Moo-moo here, and a Moo-moo there,
Here a Moo, there a Moo, everywhere a Moo-moo,
Old MacDonald had a farm, ee-aye-ee-aye-o.

Old MacDonald had a farm, ee-aye-ee-aye-o,
And on that farm he had some dogs, ee-aye-ee-aye-o,
With a Woof-woof here, and a Woof-woof there,
Here a Woof, there a Woof, everywhere a Woof-woof,
With a Baa-baa here, and a Baa-baa there,
Here a Baa, there a Baa, everywhere a Baa-baa,
With a Quack-quack here, and a Quack-quack there,
Here a Quack, there a Quack, everywhere a Quack-quack,
With a Moo-moo here, and a Moo-moo there,
Here a Moo, there a Moo, everywhere a Moo-moo,
Old MacDonald had a farm, ee-aye-ee-aye-o.

THE FARMER IN THE DELL

Age 3+   **Players Group**

Play

✿ The players form a circle and hold hands, with one player in the center, who is the farmer.

✿ As they sing, the players walk or dance around the farmer. At the end of the first verse, the farmer picks one of the others to be his wife, and the chosen one joins him in the circle.

✿ At the end of the second verse, the wife chooses a child, and so on for each verse.

✿ When patting the cheese, make sure the children are gentle.

The farmer in the dell, the farmer in the dell,
Heigh-ho, the derry-o,
The farmer's in the dell.

The farmer wants a wife, the farmer wants a wife,
Heigh-ho, the derry-o,
The farmer wants a wife.

The wife wants a child, the wife wants a child,
Heigh-ho, the derry-o,
The wife wants a child.

The child wants a nurse, the child wants a nurse,
Heigh-ho, the derry-o,
The child wants a nurse.

The nurse wants a dog, the nurse wants a dog,
Heigh-ho, the derry-o,
The nurse wants a dog.

The dog wants a cat, the dog wants a cat,
Heigh-ho, the derry-o,
The dog wants a cat.

The cat wants a rat, the cat wants a rat,
Heigh-ho, the derry-o,
The cat wants a rat.

The rat wants a cheese, the rat wants a cheese,
Heigh-ho, the derry-o,
The rat wants a cheese,

We all pat the cheese, we all pat the cheese,
Heigh-ho, the derry-o,
we all pat the cheese.

THE WHEELS ON THE BUS

Age 3+   **Players Group**

Play

❈ The players stand in a circle and perform the actions described in the verses.

❈ For the first verse, they roll their hands over each other, for the second they make engine noises, for the third they make bell-pulling actions, for the fourth they cry like babies, for the fifth they stand and sit down. Extra verses and actions can be added.

The wheels on the bus go round and round,
Round and round, round and round,
The wheels on the bus go round and round,
All through the town.

The engine on the bus goes Brrrmm-Brrrmm-Brrrmm!
Brrrmm-Brrrmm-Brrrmm!, Brrrmm-Brrrmm-Brrrmm!
The engine on the bus goes Brrrmm-Brrrmm-Brrrmm!
All through the town.

The bell on the bus goes Ding! Ding! Ding!
Ding! Ding! Ding!, Ding! Ding! Ding!
The bell on the bus goes Ding! Ding! Ding!
All through the town.

The baby on the bus goes Wahh! Wahh! Wahh!
Wahh! Wahh! Wahh!, Wahh! Wahh! Wahh!
The baby on the bus goes Wahh! Wahh! Wahh!
All through the town.

The people on the bus stand up, sit down,
Stand up, sit down, stand up, sit down,
The people on the bus stand up, sit down,
All through the town.

THIS OLD MAN

Age 3+   **Players Group**

Play

✿ The players form a circle, standing or sitting.

✿ As they sing the first line of each verse, the players hold up the appropriate number of fingers, and hold up, point to or mime the thing named, for the second line they slap their knees in time to the rhythm, and for the last line they can roll about on the floor if space allows, or rotate their hands around in front of their bodies.

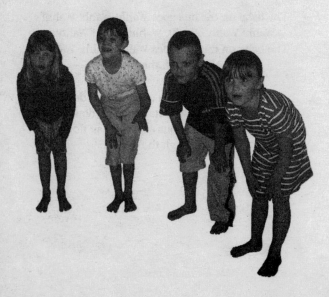

This old man, he played one, he played nick-nack on my thumb
With a nick-nack paddy-whack give the dog a bone,
This old man came rolling home.

This old man, he played two, he played nick-nack on my shoe,
With a nick-nack paddy-whack give the dog a bone,
This old man came rolling home.

This old man, he played three, he played nick-nack on my knee
With a nick-nack paddy-whack give the dog a bone,
This old man came rolling home.

This old man, he played four, he played nick-nack on my floor
With a nick-nack paddy-whack give the dog a bone,
This old man came rolling home.

This old man, he played five, he played nick-nack on a beehive
With a nick-nack paddy-whack give the dog a bone,
This old man came rolling home.

This old man, he played six, he played nick-nack
with some sticks
With a nick-nack paddy-whack give the dog a bone,
This old man came rolling home.

This old man, he played seven, he played nick-nack
up in heaven
With a nick-nack paddy-whack give the dog a bone,
This old man came rolling home.

This old man, he played eight, he played nick-nack on my gate
With a nick-nack paddy-whack give the dog a bone,
This old man came rolling home.

This old man, he played nine, he played nick-nack on the line
With a nick-nack paddy-whack give the dog a bone,
This old man came rolling home.

This old man, he played ten, he played nick-nack on my hen
With a nick-nack paddy-whack give the dog a bone,
This old man came rolling home.

MUSICAL PATTERNS

Age 5+   **Players** Teams

Equipment
A cassette player, or a musical instrument such as a piano, is needed to provide the music.

Preparation
The players are arranged into teams of equal numbers.

Play
* The music starts and the players march, or dance, around the room as they wish.
* The host calls out a shape and stops the music, whereupon the players rush to find their teammates and form the shape. The host should start with easy shapes, such as a circle and a square, and progress to more complicated ones, such as letters of the alphabet. Some suggestions are given on these pages.
* One point may be awarded in each round for the team with the best shape. The team that scores the highest number of points wins.

MUSICAL CHAIRS

Age 5+   **Players** Group

Equipment
Chairs and something to play music on.

Preparation

Chairs are placed around the room in a large circle. There should be one chair fewer than the number of players.

Play

❀ The players stand in the circle and, when the music starts, all dance around.

❀ When the music stops, each player tries to sit on a seat. The player left without a seat is eliminated.

❀ One chair is then removed from the circle and the music is restarted.

❀ The last person to stay in the game is the winner.

MUSICAL BUMPS

Age 5+   **Players Group**

This is like Musical Chairs, except that it is played without the chairs.

Equipment

Something to play music on.

Play

❀ When the music stops, players sit down on the floor. The last person to sit down is out.

❀ The last person to stay in the game is the winner.

MUSICAL NUMBERS

Age 5+   **Players Group**

Equipment
Something to play
music on.

Play
❀ The players
   march, walk
   or dance
   around the
   room as the
   music plays.
   From time to
   time, the host
   stops the music
   and calls out a
   number. If the
   number is
   three, the
   players must
   arrange them-
   selves into
groups of three. If he calls out four, then
they must form groups of four.

✹ Any players finding themselves not part of a group drop out of the game.

✹ The game ends when there are only three or four players remaining, too few with which to continue the game.

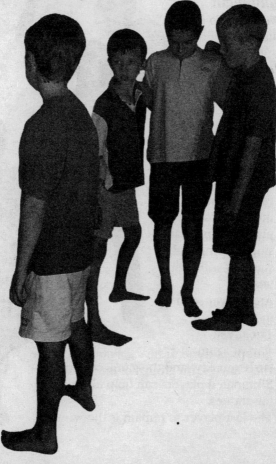

MUSICAL STATUES

Age **3+**
Players **Group**

This game is an enjoy-
able "quiet" alternative
to Musical Chairs.

Equipment
Something to play
music on.

Play
* Players dance
  around the room to
  music. When the
  music stops, the
  players immediately
  stop dancing and
  stand as still as stat-
  ues.
* Any player seen
  moving is out.
* The music is
  started again
  fairly quickly, and the game continues.
  Eliminated players can help to spot moving statues.
* The last player to remain is the winner.

PASS THE PARCEL

Age 5+   **Players Group**

Preparation

A small present is wrapped in layer after layer of paper. Each layer should be secured with thread, glue, or a rubber band. Music—to be started and stopped by someone not taking part in the game—is also needed.

Play

* Players sit in a circle and one of them holds the parcel. When the music starts, players pass the parcel around the circle to the right.

* When the music stops, whoever is holding the parcel unwraps one layer of wrapping. The music is then restarted and the parcel passed on again.

❀ The game continues in this way until someone takes off the final wrapping and so wins the present.

Picture
Games

BUTTERFLIES

Age 5+   **Players 2**

Equipment
You will need about six tubes of brightly colored oil paints, scissors, and a piece of paper for each player. This game can be quite messy.

Preparation
Fold each piece of paper in two.

Play
* Get those taking part to squeeze blobs of three different colors of paint on one half of their piece of paper (**a**). They should try to put some blobs near the crease.
* Each player should then fold the paper together, and open it out (**b**). The result should resemble a butterfly, which could be cut out.
* The results are judged and a prize awarded to the creator of the best "butterfly."

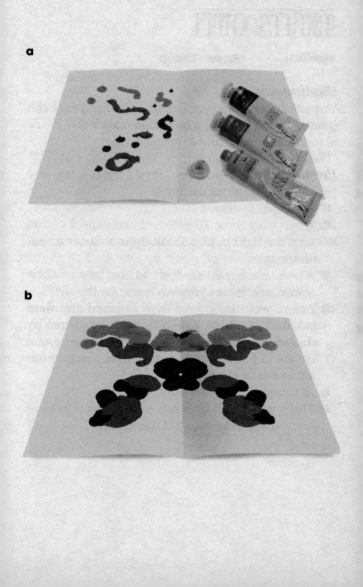

LIGHTS OUT!

Age 10+   **Players Group**

Equipment
A pencil and a piece of paper are needed for each player. A non-playing judge is also needed.

Play
❀ Make sure the players are sitting comfortably and then turn out the lights.

❀ Ask them to draw a lake.

❀ When they have all finished and expect you to turn the light back on, ask them to draw a boat on the lake.

❀ When this has been done to the best of their ability, ask them to draw a house on the shore.

❀ Again, wait until they have finished and then ask them to draw a man in the boat, a tree by the house, a fisherman by the shore, some clouds in the sky, and so on until the picture has a number of elements.

❀ At this point turn the lights back on.

❀ The winner will be whoever is judged to have created the most recognizable scene.

PICTURE CONSEQUENCES

Age 5+   **Players Group**

Aim

Players cooperate to produce a funny picture.

Play

✸ The players draw parts of an animal or a person dressed in funny clothing, according to choice. They start with the head, then fold the paper so only the neck is showing.

✸ Each person passes the paper to his or her neighbor, who draws the next section, and so on.

✸ After drawing the feet, players may write down the name of the person whom they want the figure to represent!

✸ There is no winner, the game is played for fun.

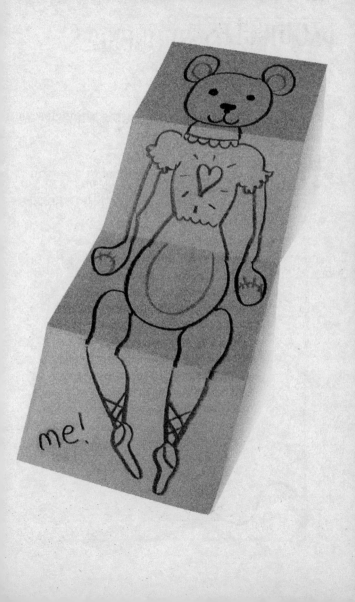

SQUIGGLES

***Age* 5–10**   ***Players* Group**

Aim
The players make drawings, using squiggles as their starting point.

Play
✻ Each player scribbles very quickly on his or her piece of paper—the more abstract the squiggle, the better.

❋ Players then exchange papers and set themselves a time limit of, for example, two minutes, in which they must use every bit of the squiggle to make a picture. Ingenuity is more important than artistic ability—the challenge is to use your squiggle inventively!

❋ There are no winners, the game is just for the fun of it.

Racing
Games

ASSAULT COURSE

Age 5+   **Players Teams**

Equipment
Lots of obstacles and varied items are needed for the course—dressing-up clothes, sacks, balls, balloons, apples, potatoes and spoons, for example.

Preparation
The objects are laid out in advance by the host along a course. Starting and finishing lines should be marked with string or chalk. Examples of suitable obstacles include a long jump, a potato and spoon dash, a box to be leaped over, a rope for six skips, a sack for jumping into the next obstacle, and an old shirt to put on.

Play
* The host first explains what has to be done at each point along the course. The object is for each team to complete the course.
* On the word "Go!" the first member of each team runs the course and must cope with every obstacle in turn, as instructed.
* Once he or she has completed the course and reaches the finishing line, the next team member can start.
* The team with all its members at the finishing line first wins.

BALLOON RACE

Age 5+   **Players Teams**

Equipment
Two balloons.

Preparation
Separate the players into two teams of equal numbers.

Play
❀ The teams form two lines, which stand side by side. The balloon is given to the front player in

each team, who passes it backward over his or her head to the next player.

❀ The balloon is passed backward along the line to the last player, who runs to the front of the line and then passes the balloon through his or her feet to the player behind.

❀ This alternating process continues until the teams revert to the positions they were in at the beginning of the game.

❀ The first team to reach its original position wins.

EGG-CUP RACE

Age 10+   **Players Teams**

Equipment
Two egg cups and a table-tennis ball are needed for each team. The egg cups should not be so large that a table-tennis ball, when placed in one, cannot be blown out.

Preparation
Players are separated into two teams. They sit on opposite sides of a table.

Play
❀ After "Go!" the first player in each team takes the egg cups and puts the table-tennis ball in the first egg-cup. The idea is to blow the ball into the next egg cup, which can be as close as the players wish to the first one.

❇ When this is achieved, table-tennis ball and egg cups are passed on to the next member of the team, who has to do the same.

❇ The first team in which everyone has managed to blow the table-tennis ball into the second egg cup is the winner.

GOING AWAY

Age 5+   **Players** Teams

Equipment

Two suitcases packed with old clothes. One will be full of female clothes and objects; the other full of male clothes and items.

Preparation

The players are arranged into two equal teams—one of males and one of females. The teams stand as far away from the suitcases as possible.

Play

❇ When they are told to start, the first player from each team hops to the suitcase containing male items if the player is female—or a case containing female items if the player is male.

❇ The players put on the clothes and, if there is any makeup, or wigs or toiletries, they should attempt to utilize these in some way. Each then picks up the suitcase and hops back to the starting line. Once there, they remove the clothes and replace them in the cases.

✿ They now hop back to the end of the room with the cases, drop them and run back to the start. The next player performs the same routine.

✿ The first team to complete the course wins.

HOOP RACE

Age 5+   **Players Teams**

Equipment
Two hoops. Alternatively, two rings made from string can be used.

Preparation
Players are divided into two teams of equal numbers.

Play
✿ The teams stand in two lines.

✿ When they are given the word "Go!" the first player takes the hoop, passes it over his or her head and steps through it, before passing it on to the player behind.

✿ This goes on down the line.

✿ When the last person in the line has stepped through the hoop, he or she runs with it to the front of the line and the game continues.

✿ The winning team is the first that has its players back in their original positions.

HURRY, WAITER!

Age 5+   **Players Teams**

Aim
Players try to keep a table-tennis ball balanced on a plate while weaving in and out of a line of their teammates.

Play
❀ Players divide into teams and stand in a line behind their leaders. Each leader is given a table-tennis ball on a plate.

❀ At the word "Go!" he weaves in and out between the players in his team as quickly as he can without dropping the ball.

* When he reaches the end of the line, he runs straight to the head of the line again and hands the plate and ball to the next player, saying "Here is your breakfast, Sir (or Madam)" as he does so.
* This procedure is repeated, with each player beginning at the head of the line and returning to his place as soon as he has handed the "breakfast" to the next player in turn.
* If a player drops the ball, he must go back to the head of the line and start again. The first team to finish wins the game.

PIGGY-BACK RACE

Age 7+   **Players Teams**

This is another race in which pairs of players try to be the first to run a course.

Play
* Players form pairs and line up at one end of the room. One player from each pair gets on the other's back to be carried.
* At the word "Go!" the pairs race to the other end of the room, where they must change places so that the carrier becomes the carried.
* They must then race back to the original end of the room. If a player touches the floor while he is being carried, that pair must start again.

PASSING THE ORANGE

Age **5+**
Players **Teams**

Aim

Seated players try to pass an
orange down the line
using their chins, or (in
an alternative version)
by using their feet!

Play

❋ Players divide into
teams and stand in
a line beside their
leaders. Each leader is
given an orange
which is tucked
between chin
and chest. On

the word "Go!" he passes the orange to the next player—neither player may use his hands. (Alternatively, the players sit side-by-side in a line on the floor and the leader, legs together, cradles the orange on his feet. He then passes it to the feet of the next player.

❀ Using either one of these ways, the orange is passed from player to player. If the orange drops on the floor, or if a player uses his hands, the orange is returned to the leader to start again.

> ❀ The first team to pass the orange down the line wins.

POTATO RACE

Age 5+   **Players** Group

Equipment
Five potatoes, two plates and one spoon are needed for each player.

Preparation
For each player, place a spoon on a plate at the starting line. Place another plate, holding five potatoes, on a line a few feet away.

Play
❀ On the word "Go!" each player has to pick up a spoon, run to the plate containing the potatoes and—using only the spoon—scoop up the first potato. Each now runs back to the starting line and deposits the potato on the plate there.

❀ This procedure continues until all five potatoes have been successfully carried to the plate at the starting line.

❀ Players must only use one hand to carry the spoon. If a potato drops onto the ground, it must be scooped up again into the spoon.

❀ The winner is the first player to transport all their potatoes from one plate to the other.

THREE-LEGGED RACE

Age 5+   **Players** Group

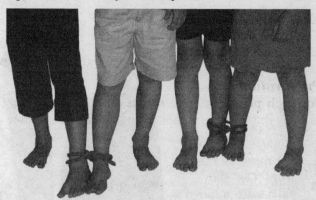

Aim
Pairs of players try to be the first to run from one end of the room to the other.

Equipment
A scarf is needed to tie together the legs of the players in each pair.

Play
❀ Players form pairs and line up at one end of the room. The scarves are used to tie the right leg of one of the players in the pair to the left leg of his or her partner. At the word "Go!" pairs race to the other end of the room.

TORTOISE RACE

Age 5+
Players Group

Aim
Each player tries to be the last to finish.

Play
❀ Players line up along one side of the room. At the word "Go!" they each start to move across the room as slowly as possible. They must head straight for the opposite wall.

❀ A player is disqualified if he or she stops moving or changes direction.

WOOL TANGLES

Age 5+   *Players* **Teams**

Aim
Teams of four players try to be first to untangle balls of yarn wrapped around chairs.

Preparation
A chair and four differently colored balls of yarn are needed for each team.

Play
❋ Players form into teams of four. Each team is given four balls of yarn and a chair.

❋ Teams are then allowed about one minute in which to tangle their yarn around their chairs. They are not allowed to lift up their chairs or to make deliberate knots in the yarn.

❋ At the end of the time limit, the organizer calls "Stop!" and teams must move around to a different chair.

❋ At the word "Go!" teams start to disentangle the yarn from their new chair. Each player winds one of the balls of yarn. Players are not allowed to pick up the chair or deliberately break the yarn.

❋ The game is won by the first team to untangle the yarn into four separate balls.

Dice Games

Dice games were played in ancient times and remain universally popular.

Dice

A standard modern die is a regular cube, with the six sides numbered with dots from 1 to 6. Any two opposing sides add up to 7.

Odds

With one true die, each face has an equal chance of landing face up. With two dice thrown together, some scores are more likely than others because there are more ways in which they can be made.

BEETLE

Age 8+   **Players 2**

Equipment

1) One die, either an ordinary one or a special "beetle die" marked B (body), H (head), L (legs), E (eye), F (feeler) and T (tail);
2) a simple drawing of a beetle as a guide, showing its various parts and (when an ordinary die is used) their corresponding numbers (1 = B; 2 = H; 3 = L; 4 = E; 5 = F; 6 = T);
3) a pencil and a piece of paper for each player.

Aim

Each player, by throwing the die, tries to complete his drawing of the beetle.

Play

❀ Each player throws the die once only in each round. Each player must begin by throwing a B (or a 1); this permits the player to draw the body.

❀ When this has been drawn, he or she can throw for other parts of the beetle that can be joined to the body. An H or a 2 must be thrown to link the head to the body before the feelers (F or 5) and eyes (E or 4) can be added.

❀ Each eye or feeler requires its own throw. A throw of L or 3 permits the player to add three legs to one side of the body.

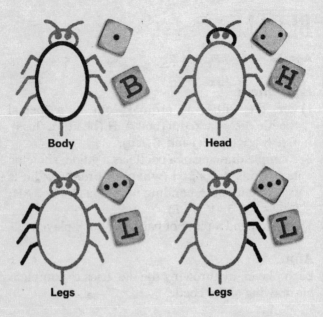

Body

Head

Legs

Legs

✿ A further throw of L or 3 is necessary for the other three legs. Sometimes it is agreed that a player may continue to throw during a turn for as long as he or she throws parts of the body that can be used.

✿ The first to complete his or her beetle scores 13 points and is the winner. The 13 points represent the total of each part of the beetle (body, head, tail, two feelers, two eyes and six legs).

Continuing play

When a series of games is played, each player counts one point for every part of the beetle he or she has been able to draw, and cumulative scores

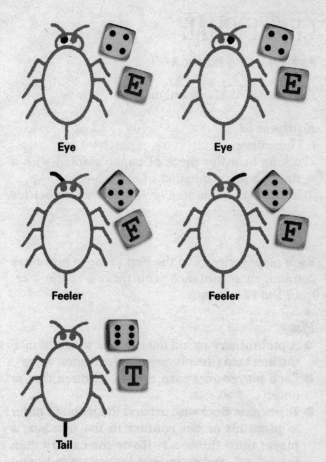

Eye

Eye

Feeler

Feeler

Tail

are carried from round to round. The winner is the player with the highest score at the end of the series or the first to reach a previously agreed total score.

CENTENNIAL

Age 10+   **Players 2**

Also known as Martinetti or Ohio.

Equipment
1) Three dice;
2) a long board or piece of paper marked with a row of boxes numbered 1 to 12;
3) a distinctive counter or some other object for each player.

Aim
Each player tries to be the first to move his or her counter, in accordance with throws of the dice, from 1 to 12 and back.

Play
❋ A preliminary round determines who will take the first turn (the player with the highest score).
❋ Each player on a turn throws all three dice at once.
❋ Turns pass clockwise around the table. In order to place his or her counter in the first box, a player must throw a 1. He or she can try then for a 2, a 3, and so on, box by box up to 12 and back again. He or she can make any number with one or more dice. For example, a 3 can be scored with one 3, a 1 and a 2, or with three 1s. It is possible to move through more than one box on a single throw. For example, a throw of

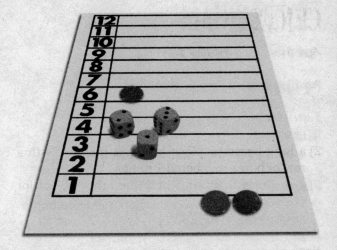

1, 2, 3 would not only take him or her through the first three boxes, but on through the fourth (1 + 3 = 4), to the fifth (2 + 3 = 5) and finally the sixth (1 + 2 + 3 = 6). Other players' throws must be watched constantly. If a player throws a number he or she needs but overlooks and does not use it, that number may be claimed by any other player, who must do this as soon as the dice are passed and must be able to use it at once.

✿ The first player to get to 12 and back wins.

CHICAGO

Age 8+   **Players 2**

Equipment
Two dice are used.

Aim
To score each of 11 combinations in turn.

Play
❋ The game is based on the 11 possible combinations of the two dice—2, 3, 4, 5, 6, 7, 8, 9, 10, 11 and 12—and so consists of 11 rounds.

❋ Each player in turn rolls the dice once in each round. During the first round, he or she will try to make a total of 2, during the second, a total of 3, and so on, up to 12. Each time the player is successful, that number of points is added to his or her score. For example, if he or she is shooting for 5 and throws a total of 5, the player gains 5 points. If he or she fails to make the desired number, he or she scores nothing on that throw.

❋ The player with the highest score after the 11 rounds is the winner.

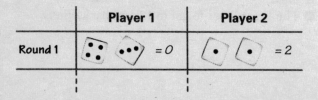

	Player 1	**Player 2**
Round 1	= 0	= 2

	Player 1	Player 2
Round 2	= 0	= 0
Round 3	= 4	= 0
Round 4	= 0	= 5
Round 5	= 6	= 6
Round 6	= 0	= 0
Round 7	= 0	= 0
Round 8	= 9	= 0
Round 9	= 10	= 0
Round 10	= 0	= 11
Round 11	= 0	= 12
TOTAL	29	36

DROP DEAD

Age 8+   **Players 2+**

Equipment
1) Five dice;
2) paper on which to record players' scores.

Aim
Players aim to make the highest total score.

Play
❀ At his or her turn, each player begins by rolling the five dice. Each time he or she makes a throw that does not contain a 2 or a 5, he or she scores the total spot value of that throw and is entitled to another throw with all five dice.

❀ Whenever a player makes a throw containing a 2 or a 5, nothing is scored for that throw and any die or dice that showed a 2 or a 5 must be excluded from any further throws. A player's turn continues until his or her last remaining die shows a 2 or a 5—at which point he or she "drops dead" and play passes to the next player.

Example of play

throw 1

= 0 points

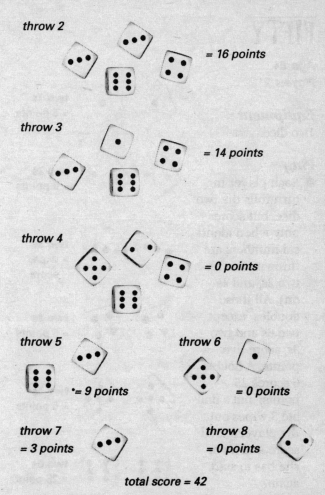

throw 2 = 16 points

throw 3 = 14 points

throw 4 = 0 points

throw 5 •= 9 points

throw 6 = 0 points

throw 7 = 3 points

throw 8 = 0 points

total score = 42

✱ The player who gains the highest score wins. The total score in the example shown here is 42 points.

FIFTY

Age 8+
Players 2

Equipment
Two dice.

Play

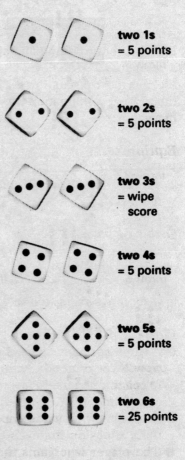

two 1s
= 5 points

two 2s
= 5 points

two 3s
= wipe
  score

two 4s
= 5 points

two 5s
= 5 points

two 6s
= 25 points

❋ Each player in turn rolls the two dice, but scores only when identical numbers are thrown (two 1s, two 2s, and so on). All these doubles, except two 6s and two 3s, score five points. A double 6 scores 25 points; and a double 3 wipes out the player's total score and he or she has to start again.

❋ The winner is the first player to reach the score of 50 points.

GENERAL

Age 10+   **Players 2**

Aim
Each player or partnership aims to win by scoring a "big general" (see Five of a kind, page 136) or by scoring most points for the 10 general combinations. Each combination may be scored only once in a game.

Equipment
1) Five dice;
2) a score sheet showing combinations and players' names.

Order of play
Determined by a preliminary round in which each player rolls the dice once. The player with the lowest spot score shoots first, the player with the next lowest score second, and so on.

Play
✤ A game normally consists of 10 turns ("frames") per player, but ends immediately if any player rolls a "big general." Players take it in turn to roll each frame.

✤ Each player may roll the dice once, twice, or three times during each frame. If, on the first throw, the player fails to make a combination that he or she wishes to score, he or she may pick up all or any of the dice for a second roll.

But the value of any combination he or she now rolls is diminished, and a "big general" now becomes a "small general."

❀ After the second roll the player may again, if he or she wishes, pick up all or any of the dice for a third roll.

❀ After the third roll, he or she must state which combination he or she is scoring.

❀ Play then passes to the next player.

❀ If the game runs its full course of 10 frames, the player with the highest score wins.

Aces wild

"Aces" (1s) may be counted as 2 or as 6 if one or both of these are needed to complete a Straight—but not as any other number or for any other purpose.

Combinations

Numbers 1 to 6 Score their spot values.

Straight Either 1, 2, 3, 4, 5 or 2, 3, 4, 5, 6 scores 25 points if made on the first throw, but only 20 points if made on the second or third throws. Only one straight is scored.

Full house Three of a kind and two of a kind score 35 points on the first throw but only 30 points on the second or third throws.

Four of a kind Scores 45 points on the first throw, but only 40 points on the second or third throws.

Five of a kind If made on the first throw it ranks

Player 1	**Player 2**
frame 1	
throw 1	*throw 1*

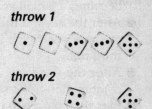

| *throw 2* | *throw 2* |

| = straight = 20 points | = straight = 20 points |

| *frame 2* | |
| *throw 1* | *throw 1* |

| *throw 2* | *throw 2* |

| | *throw 3* |

| = full house = 30 points | = fours = 12 points |

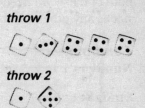

as the "big general" and immediately wins the game. Made on the second or third throws it is a "small general" and scores 60 points.

Player 1	Player 2

frame 3

throw 1

throw 1

throw 2

throw 2

throw 3

throw 3

= 3s = 6 points

= full house = 30 points

	Player 1	Player 2
1s		
2s		
3s	6	
4s		12
5s		
6s		
Straight	20	20
Full house	30	30
Four of a kind		
Five of a kind		

DOUBLE CAMEROON

Age 10+ **Players 2**

This game is like General, but with important differences.

Equipment
Ten dice.

Play
❀ After a player has rolled the dice for the third time in each turn, he or she divides them into two groups of five, and then allots the score of each group to one of the 10 combinations in the game. So in the course of a game, each player has five turns.

Combinations
Numbers 1 to 6 Score their spot values.

Full house Scores its spot value.

Little Cameroon 1, 2, 3, 4, 5 scores 21 points.

Big Cameroon 2, 3, 4, 5, 6 scores 30 points.

Five of a kind Scores 50 points.

NB: Unlike in General, a score does not decrease if the combination is made on a second or third throw.

GOING TO BOSTON

Age 8+   **Players 2**

Also known as Newmarket or Yankee Grab.

Equipment
Three dice.

Aim
Players try to win as many of an agreed number of rounds as they can.

Play
- Each player in turn rolls the three dice together.
- After the first roll, the player leaves the dice showing the highest number on the table then rolls the other two again. Of these, the die with the highest number is also left on the table and the remaining die is rolled again.
- This completes the player's throw: the total of the three dice is his or her score.
- When all players have thrown, the player with the highest score wins the round. Ties are settled by further rolling.
- The player who wins the most rounds is the winner. Alternatively, each player can contribute counters to a pool that is won at the end of each game.

Variation
A variation known as Multiplication is played like

Going to Boston, but with one important difference. When each player has completed a turn, his or her score is the sum of the spot values of the first two dice retained, multiplied by that of the third. For example, if the player's first throw is 5, the second throw 4, and the final throw 6, the score will be 54: (5 + 4) x 6.

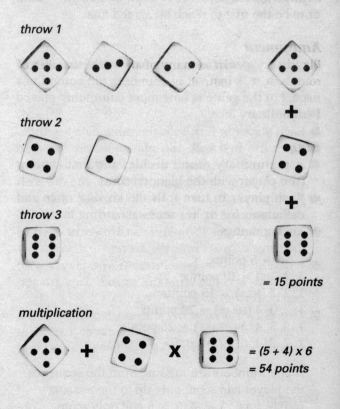

throw 1

throw 2

throw 3

= 15 points

multiplication

= (5 + 4) x 6
= 54 points

HEARTS

Age 10+   **Players 2**

Aim

Players try to score more than their opponents over an agreed series of rounds, or a single round, or to be the first to reach an agreed total.

Equipment

Six dice. Special dice marked with the letters H, E, A, R, T, S instead of numbers are sometimes used, but the game is now more commonly played with ordinary dice.

Play

❀ A preliminary round decides the first shooter (the player with the highest score).

❀ Each player in turn rolls the six dice once and calculates his or her score according to the following ratings:

1 (H) = 5 points;
1, 2 (HE) = 10 points;
1, 2, 3 (HEA) = 15 points;
1, 2, 3, 4 (HEAR) = 20 points;
1, 2, 3, 4, 5 (HEART) = 25 points;
1, 2, 3, 4, 5, 6 (HEARTS) = 35 points.

If any numbers are missing from the sequence, the player can score only up to the missing number: i.e., 1, 2, 3, 5, 5, 6 will only score

15 points; 2, 3, 4, 4, 5, 6 will score nothing at all. If a double (two dice of the same spot value) or a treble appears in the throw, only one of the numbers or letters counts. But if three 1s (or Hs) are thrown, the player's whole score is wiped out and he or she has to start again.

✴ The player with the highest score wins.

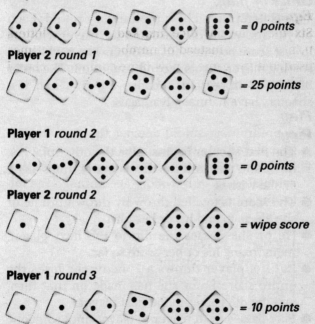

Player 1 *round 1*

= 0 points

Player 2 *round 1*

= 25 points

Player 1 *round 2*

= 0 points

Player 2 *round 2*

= wipe score

Player 1 *round 3*

= 10 points

Player 2 *round 3*

= 0 points

PĪG

Age 8+   **Players 2**

Aim

Using one die, players try to reach an agreed total score (usually 100) before the other players.

Order of play

This is determined by a preliminary round. Each player throws the die once and the player with the lowest score becomes first shooter. The next lowest scoring player shoots second, and so on. The order of play is important because the first and last shooters have natural advantages.

Play

* The first shooter begins. Like the other players, he or she may roll the die as many times as he or she wishes.
* The score is totalled throw by throw until he or she elects to end his or her turn.
* He or she passes the die to the next player, memorizing his or her score so far.
* But if a player throws a 1, he or she loses the entire score he or she has made on that turn, and the die passes to the next player.
* Play passes from player to player until someone reaches the total score agreed.

Given a little luck, the first shooter is the player most likely to win. But his or her advantage can be counteracted by other players continuing until they have had the same number of turns. The last shooter still has the advantage of knowing the scores made by all his or her opponents. Provided a player does not roll a 1, he or she can continue throwing until all those scores are beaten. The fairest way of playing the game is to organize it as a series, with each player in turn becoming first shooter.

❁ The winner is the first player to reach the previously agreed total score.

Player 1	Player 2	Player 3	Player 4

Player 3: **out**

Player 2: **stops, scores 21**

Player 4: **stops, scores 23**

Player 1: **out**

ROUND THE CLOCK

Age 8+ **Players 2**

Aim

Players try to throw 1 to 12 in the correct sequence.

Equipment

Two dice.

Play

✤ Players throw both dice once in each turn. From 1 to 6, a player can score with either one of the two dice or with both of them—e.g., a throw of 3 and 1 can be counted as 3, 1 or 4. It is also possible at this stage to score twice on one throw, e.g., if a player needs 2 and throws a 2 and a 3 he or she can count both of these numbers. From 7 to 12, however, a player will obviously need

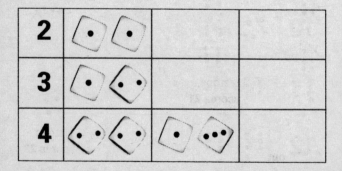

the combined spot values of both dice to score.
The table shows the combinations possible.
❋ The winner is the first to complete the correct
sequence.

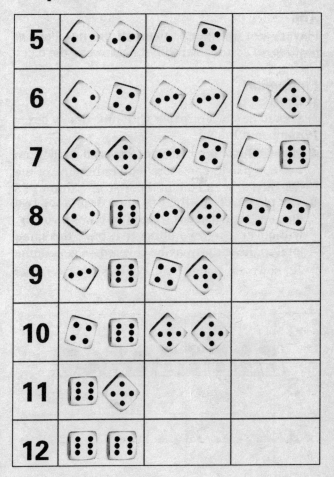

SHUT THE BOX

Age 8+   **Players 2**

Aim
Players aim to cover as many of the numbers as possible, in accordance with the throws of the dice.

Equipment
1) Two dice;
2) a board or sheet of paper with nine drawn boxes numbered 1 to 9;
3) nine counters used to cover the boxes in play.

Play
❋ The player taking the first turn throws the two dice and then decides which two boxes he or she will cover. Any two boxes that have the same total as the throw may be covered—e.g., a throw

of 5 and 3 (total 8) would allow the player to cover 5 and 3, 4 and 4 or 6 and 2.

❀ The same player then throws the two dice again and tries to cover another two boxes. He or she is not allowed to use combinations involving numbers that he has already covered. In the example, with the 8 covered (**a**) and two sixes thrown, only 9 and 3 or 7 and 5 could be covered (**b**).

❀ A player's turn continues until he or she is unable to make use of a combination from his or her latest throw. (Note that as the two dice must be used for every throw a player with only the 1 uncovered cannot continue.) All the uncovered numbers are then added up and become the player's penalty score.

❀ Play then passes to the next player.

❀ The winner is the player with the lowest penalty score from uncovered boxes.

b

TWENTY-ONE

Age 10+   **Players 2**

Equipment
One die, paper, pencil and a box of matches (or several counters).

Play
❋ Each player is given an equal number of matches (or counters). They all contribute one to the "bank." One player is chosen to start off.

❋ The player rolls the die as many times as he or she likes, trying to get as close to a total of 21 as possible. At any stage, the player can "stick," and the total is recorded. For example, if a player has scored 19 after a few throws, the chances are that the next throw will take the score to over 21, so the player may decide to "stick" with what he or she has got.

❋ The other players then make their attempts to score 21. Any player throwing a number that takes the total over 21 goes "bust."

❋ At the end of each round, the player with the highest total, not exceeding 21, takes all the matches in the bank. Players who score the same amount can either share the winnings or have a play-off to decide who takes them.

❋ After a few rounds, unlucky—or unskillful—players may run out of matches. They must then drop out of the game.

✤ The game can continue for a fixed period of time, after which the player with the highest number of matches will be the winner. Alternatively, the first player to amass a certain number of matches may be declared the winner.

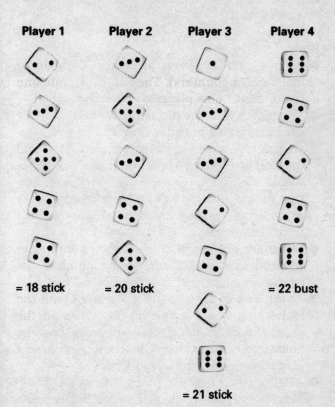

Player 1	Player 2	Player 3	Player 4
= 18 stick	= 20 stick		= 22 bust

= 21 stick

Pick Up
Sticks

PICK UP STICKS

Age 5+

This game, which originated in China, is also called Spellicans. Players try their skill at removing straws or small sticks from a pile, one at a time and without disturbing any of their neighbors. Any number of players can take part.

Equipment

Pick Up Sticks is played with a set of about 30 thin strips of wood or plastic. These strips, called pick up sticks, have carved heads representing animals, people, etc. There is also a carved hook for moving the strips.

Start of play

The order of play is determined by the throw of a die or some other means. The last person in the playing order then takes all the pick up sticks in one hand and drops them onto the table or floor. He must not interfere with any pick up stick after it has left his hand.

Play

✢ At his or her turn, each player takes the carved hook and attempts to remove a pick up stick from the pile without disturbing any of the others. Once a player has started moving a particular pick up stick, he or she is not permitted to transfer the attack to a different pick up stick.

❋ If the player successfully removes a pick up stick from the pile, he or she keeps it and tries to remove another pick up stick from the pile. A player's turn continues until a pick up stick other than the one being attacked is disturbed.

❋ Play continues in this way until all the pick up sticks have been taken.

❋ Each pick up stick has a points value, and a game is won by the player with the highest score. Pick up sticks that are generally fairly easy to move have a low value, and more elaborate and difficult to move pick up sticks have a correspondingly higher value.

LAST MATCH

Ages 5–10　　***Players 2***

Preparation
A box of about 50 matches is needed, and they should be struck first to eliminate any risk of children doing so.

Aim
To be able to pick up the last match.

Play
❀ Each player decides on a number between 1 and 10—this is the maximum number of matches he may pick up in any round.
❀ The matches are tipped in a heap, and players pick up as many matches as they wish, within their limit.
❀ They continue until all the matches have been picked up.
❀ The player who picks up the last match wins.

SQUAYLES

Ages 5–10　　　*Players 2*

Preparation
As with the other matchstick games, the matches should be struck and extinguished before being used. Any number of matches are arranged in a pattern of squares.

Aim
To be able to pick up the last match.

Play
❀ The players take turns to pick up matches. They may take one or two at a time, provided the two are next to each other, though they do not have to be in a straight line.
❀ The winner is the player who picks up the last match.

Start of play

Tiddlywinks

TIDDLYWINKS

Age 5+ **Players 2**

In the standard game of Tiddlywinks, each player attempts to put small discs or "winks" into a cup by shooting them with a larger disc called a "shooter." Variations include games based on sports such as tennis and golf.

Equipment
Each player usually has a shooter and four winks. A target cup is also needed. Winks and shooters must be slightly pliable and are commonly made of bone or plastic. Winks are usually about 0.5 in (about 1.5 cm) and shooters about 1 in (2.5 cm) in diameter. Each player's winks and shooters should be of a different color.

shooters

winks

Target cups are made of plastic, wood, or glass and are about 1.5 in (4 cm) across and 1–2 in (2.5–5 cm) high.

Playing area
Games are played on the floor or on a table. Any shape of table may be used but a square or round one is best if there are more than two players. The table should be covered with a thick cloth or piece of felt.

STANDARD TIDDLYWINKS

Shooting

A player shoots a wink by stroking and then pressing the edge of the shooter against the top edge of the wink and so making the wink jump into the air. A wink is shot from where it lies after the player's previous turn.

Play

* The cup is placed in the center of the playing area, and each player places his or her winks in a line in front of him.
* Order of play is often decided by a preliminary shot—first shot of the game going to the player who gets his or her wink nearest the cup.
* Play is then usually clockwise around the players. Each player shoots one wink in a turn plus one extra shot each time he or she gets a wink into the cup. Any wink that is partly covered by another is out of play. A player whose wink is covered by an opponent's wink must either wait until the opponent moves his or her wink or must attempt to remove the opponent's wink by hitting it with one of his or her own winks. Any wink that stops against the side of the cup is out of play until it is knocked level onto the table by another wink. A wink that is shot off the table does not go out of play. It must be replaced on the table at the point where it went off.

❉ Tiddlywinks may be scored in two ways:
  a) players count the number of games they win;
  b) players score one point for each wink in the cup.
❉ The game is won by the first player to get all his or her tiddlywinks in the cup.

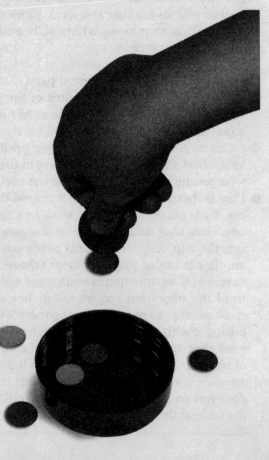

TARGET TIDDLYWINKS

This involves shooting winks at numbered targets. A typical layout is a target with concentric circles each worth a different set number of points.

Play

✹ Target Tiddlywinks is played in the same way as the standard game except that:

   a) players score a set number of points for landing their winks on different parts of the target (a wink touching two scoring areas always scores the lower number);

   b) a wink may not be shot again once it has landed on any part of the target, but may be knocked by another wink.

✹ The player with the highest score wins. This player has scored 50 + 10 + 5 + 5 = 70 points.

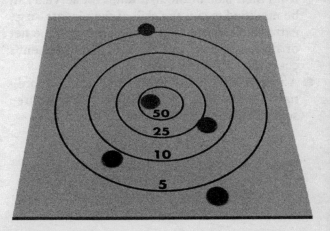

TIDDLYWINKS TENNIS

Preparation

The lines of a tennis court should be marked on the floor or the tiddlywinks cloth. (Dimensions for the court should be varied to suit the skill of the players and the height of the net.) An improvised net can be made with folded paper or card, or with a row of books.

Play

* Players shoot a wink back and forth over the net, gaining points whenever their opponents fail to get the wink over the net or shoot it so that it goes outside the limits of the court. The game can be played by two players (singles) or four players (doubles). In the doubles version, partners take alternate turns to shoot the wink from their side of the net. Rules for service can be modified to suit the skill of the players—e.g., extra shots allowed to get the wink over the net or no restrictions on where in the opponent's court the wink must land.

* A match is scored in games and sets as in ordinary tennis, with the first player to win three sets taking the match.

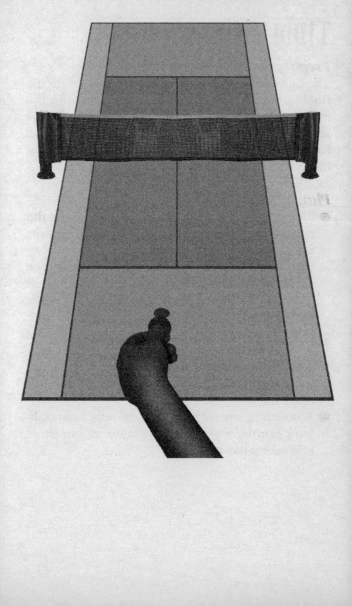

Spoken Word Games

ALL'S WELL THAT ENDS WELL

Age 10+ **Players** Group

Play

❀ Players must first choose a category—for example, food, places, animals or famous sports stars.

❀ The first player says a word from that category. If food is chosen, she might say "eggs."

❀ The next player then has to name a food that begins with the last letter of the previous word. So he might respond with "salami."

❀ The next player could say "ice cream," and so on.

❀ Players who cannot think of a new food, who answer with a food that has already been said, or answer with a word that is not in the correct category, drop out. Players can make it difficult for one another by saying a food that ends with an awkward letter.

❀ The winner is the last player left after the others have been eliminated.

EGGS
SALAMI
ICE CREAM
MERINGUE
ENDIVE
E?

ANIMAL, VEGETABLE OR MINERAL

Ages 5–10   *Players* Group

Sometimes called Twenty Questions, this game is one of the oldest and most familiar word-guessing games.

Aim
Players try to guess an object thought of by one of the others.

Play
❀ One of the players thinks of an object. It may be general (e.g., "a ship"), specific (e.g., "the Lusitania"), or a feature (e.g., "the bridge of the Lusitania").

❀ He or she then tells the others the composition of his chosen object (i.e., animal, vegetable or mineral). The three categories may be defined as follows:

1) animal: all forms of animal life or anything of animal origin, e.g., a centipede, a tortoiseshell button;

2) vegetable: all forms of vegetable life or anything of vegetable origin, e.g., a wooden cotton reel, a carrot;

3) mineral: anything inorganic or of inorganic origin, e.g., glass, a car. Objects are often a

combination of categories, for example, a can of beer or a leather shoe.

✿ The other players then ask up to 20 questions to try to guess the object. They should ask questions of a general nature rather than make random guesses, until they feel confident that they are near to knowing the object.

✿ As each question is put to the player, he or she must reply either "Yes" or "No," or "I don't know," as appropriate.

✿ The first player to guess the object correctly may choose an object for a new round of play. If no one has guessed the object by the time 20 questions have been asked, the players are told what it was, and the same person may choose an object for the next round or—if two teams are playing—a person in the other team may choose.

BOTTICELLI

Age 10+   *Players* **Group**

Aim

Players try to guess the identity of a personality by asking questions.

Play

✿ One player chooses the name of a famous person and tells the other players the initial of the name. For example, he or she might say "M" for Madonna.

❀ Taking turns, each player must think of a character whose name begins with that letter, and describe the character without naming the person he or she has in mind. If he or she thought of Mickey Mouse, he would ask, "Are you a Walt Disney character?"

❀ If the first player recognizes the description, he or she answers, "No, I am not Mickey Mouse," and another player may make a guess.

❀ If the first player does not recognize the description, however, the player who gave it may then ask a direct question that will give him or her and the other players a lead, such as "Are you in the entertainment business?"

❀ The first player must give a truthful "Yes" or "No" reply. The first person to guess the personality wins the round and may choose the next character. If nobody succeeds in guessing the personality after a reasonable length of time, the first player tells them the answer and may choose again for the new round.

BUZZ

Age **10+**   *Players* **Group**

This game should be played as briskly as possible for maximum enjoyment.

Aim

To count numbers remembering which ones to replace with the word "Buzz."

Play

✿ The players sit in a circle.

✿ One player calls out "One," the next player "Two," the next "Three," and so on.

✿ As soon as the number five, or any multiple of five, is reached, the players must say "Buzz." If the number contains a five but is not a multiple of five, only part of it is replaced by buzz. (For example, 52 would be "Buzz two.") If a player forgets to say "Buzz" or hesitates too long, he or she drops out.

✿ The last player remaining in the game is the winner.

Buzz

1·2·3·4·Buzz 6·7·8·9·Buzz

Variations

A variation is called Fizz. This is played exactly like Buzz, except that players say "Fizz" for seven or multiples of seven. Another variation, Buzz-Fizz, combines the two games, so that 57, for example, becomes Buzz-Fizz.

Fizz

Buzz-Fizz

CRAZY CHEF

Ages 5–10   **Players Group**

Preparation

Players form a circle, with one of them standing in the center, who acts as the "chef."

Play

* The player in the center must point to someone in the circle, saying—for example—"I only like the letter M. What shall I cook for supper?"
* The player who has been pointed at now has to suggest something suitable for supper that contains that letter—for example, meat or hamburgers. Anything suggested must be edible and cooked, rather than eaten raw. If the player pointed at fails to come up with a suitable "meal," he or she is out and leaves the circle.
* After each turn, the "chef" asks for suggestions using another letter, but X, Y and Z are not allowed.
* "Meals" cannot be suggested more than once. The game continues in this way until only one player is left.
* The last player left wins.

GHOSTS

Age 10+　　　　**Players Group**

Aim

Players take it in turns to contribute a letter to an unstated word while trying to avoid completing any word.

Play

* The first player begins by thinking of any word (e.g., rabbit) and calls out the first letter (R).
* The next player then thinks of a word beginning with R (e.g., rescue) and calls out its second letter (E).
* Play then continues in this way until one of the players is unable to contribute a letter that does not complete a word.
* Whenever a player completes a word—and the other players notice—that player loses a "life." This is true even if the player completes a word by accident because they were thinking of another word.
* If a player is unable to think of a suitable word, they may try to bluff their way out of the situation by calling out a letter of an imaginary word.
* If, however, they hesitate for too long or the other players suspect that they have no particular word in mind, they may challenge the player. The challenged player must state the word and if they cannot do so lose a life. If the explanation is satisfactory, however, the challenger loses a life.

Whenever a player loses a first life they become "a third of a ghost." Losing a second life makes them "two-thirds of a ghost," and if a player loses a third life they become a whole ghost and must drop out of the game.

✿ The game is won by the player who manages to survive the longest.

R (abbit)

R E (scue)

R E P (lica)

R E P E (at)

R E P E A (t)

R E P E A L

I LOVE MY LOVE

Age 10+   **Players Group**

Aim

Players think of an adjective beginning with each letter of the alphabet to complete a given statement.

Play

❀ The first player starts by saying, "I love my love because he [or she] is . . ." using any adjective beginning with A.

❀ The next person repeats the phrase, but his or her adjective must begin with B, the next person's with C, and so on through the alphabet. Alternatively, each player must make a different statement as well as using an adjective with a different letter. Examples of suitable statements are: Her name is (Anna), she lives in (Arnhem), and I shall give her (an aardvark).

❀ Players may write down the chosen statements if they wish, but there must be no hesitation over the answers.

❀ Any player who hesitates or gives an incorrect answer drops out of the game.

❀ The winner is the last person left in.

Variation

A similar game, known as A Was An Apple Pie, involves players thinking of a verb instead of an adjective. The first player says: "A was an apple pie. A ate it," and other players might add "B baked it," "C chose it," "D dropped it," and so on.

Adjectives for playing I Love My Love

A attractive, attentive, alluring, appreciative
B bashful, beautiful, brainy, burlesque
C charming, cute, courteous, courageous
D dainty, dextrous, daring, different
E eccentric, effeminate, errant, extravagant
F fair, fun, flamboyant, forceful
G gallant, gorgeous, groovy, generous
H happy, hilarious, hearty, humble
I ingenious, illustrious, imaginative, intelligent
J jaunty, jolly, jubilant, joyful
K keen, kind, knowledgeable, kooky
L lenient, loyal, lively, lavish
M mad, mischievous, modish, mysterious
N natty, notorious, noble, nice
O obedient, optimistic, open-minded, outspoken
P polite, patient, prestigious, profound
Q quiet, qualitative, queenly, quick
R rebellious, resolute, resourceful, responsible
S silly, sagacious, sedate, skillful
T timid, thin, thoughtful, tolerant
U upstanding, understanding, unselfish, unflappable
V voracious, virtuous, vivacious, valiant
W warm, wholesome, wise, wonderful
X —
Y young, youthful, yummy
Z zany, zappy, zealous, zippy

I SPY

Ages 5–10   **Players Group**

Aim

Each player tries to be the first to guess which visible object one of them has spied.

Play

❋ Two or more people can play, and one of them is chosen to start.

❋ He or she says, "I spy, with my little eye, something beginning with . . ." and gives the first letter of an object that he or she has secretly chosen and that is visible to all the players. (They may have to turn their heads in order to see the object, but they should not need to move about.) For example, if the player chose a vase, he or she would give the letter V or, if a two-word object was chosen, the first letter of each word (e.g., PF for picture frame). If the player chooses an object, such as a chair, of which there may be more than one in the room, the other players must guess the particular chair he or she has in mind.

❋ The game ends as soon as someone has spotted the object that was chosen—he or she may then spy the next object.

Variation

I Spy may be played by very young children if colors rather than first letters are given. For example,
a player may say, "I spy, with my little eye, something red," and the others then look for the red
object that he or she has in mind.

•

I WENT ON A TRIP

Age 10+   **Players Group**

Aim
Players try to remember and repeat a growing list of items.

Play
❀ One of the players chooses an article—for example an umbrella—and says, "I went on a trip and took my umbrella."

❀ The next player repeats that sentence and adds a second item after "umbrella." In this way the players gradually build up a list of articles.

❀ Each time his or her turn comes, a player repeats the list and adds another item. Whenever a player cannot repeat the list correctly, the list is closed and the next player in the group begins a new list.

Variation
A variation known as City of Boston is very similar to I Went on a Trip, but players must add to a list of items for sale. Thus the first player might say "I shall sell you a bunch of violets when you come to the City of Boston." The other players then repeat that sentence in turn and add an item that he or she will sell.

I WENT SHOPPING

Age 10+   **Players Group**

Play

❀ The first player begins by saying something like:
"I went shopping and I bought some apples" (the
first item must begin with the letter "A").

❀ The next
player must
add some-
thing begin-
ning with
"B" to the
list. For
example: "I
went shop-
ping and I
bought
some
apples
and some
bread."
The
whole list
must be
repeated
in the
course of
each
round.

❀ The third player might add "carrots" to the list. If a player gets the list wrong, or cannot think of an item beginning with the next letter of the alphabet, he or she must drop out of the game.

❀ The winner is the last player left in the game.

INITIAL ANSWERS

Age 10+   **Players** Group

Aim
To be the last remaining person in the game.

Play
* The players sit in a circle and one of them starts by thinking of any letter of the alphabet (e.g., S).
* He or she must then think of a three-letter word beginning with that letter and give a definition of the word; for example "S plus two letters is a father's child."
* The second person in the circle has to try to guess the word ("son"), and he or she then thinks of a word of four letters also beginning with S. He or she might choose "soup" and define it as "S plus three letters makes a tasty start to a meal" for the person sitting next to him or her to guess.
* This next person, after guessing the word correctly, must think of a five-letter word—perhaps "snail"—defining it as "S plus four letters carries a house on its back."
* The game continues in this way, with each person having to think of a word beginning with the chosen letter, and each word having one letter more than the previous word. Any player who fails to think of an appropriate word, or who fails to guess a word, must drop out.
* The last person left in the game is the winner. A different letter of the alphabet should be chosen for the next round.

INITIAL LETTERS

***Age* 10+   *Players* Group**

Aim
To be the last remaining person in the game.

Play
✺ The players sit in a circle.

✺ One of them puts a question—it may be as far-fetched as he or she likes—to the others.

✺ Each of them in turn must reply with a two-word answer, beginning with the initials of his or her names. Players have only five seconds in which to think of an answer. For example, if the question was, "What is your favorite food?" Brian Richards could reply, "Peanut butter," and Rosie Collins might say, "Cheese sandwich." When all the players have answered, the second player asks a question. Any player who fails to answer after five seconds or who gives a wrong answer drops out of the game.

✺ The winner is the last person to stay in.

Question: What is your favorite food?

BRIAN RICHARDS	Peanut butter
ROSIE COLLINS	Cheese sandwich
JAMES DAY	Jelly doughnuts
DANIEL BENNETT	Cookies

MY FATHER KEEPS A GROCER'S SHOP

Ages 5–10 **Players** Group

Aim

To guess the right word.

Play

✸ The players sit in a group.

✸ The first one chosen begins, "My father keeps a grocer's shop, and in it he sells . . ." Instead of saying the complete word, the player just gives the first letter. If he or she was thinking of "Carrots," he or she would say "C."

✸ The other players now try to guess what the word is.

✸ The first to guess correctly wins the round and becomes the next to think of a word.

ONE MINUTE, PLEASE

Age 10+   **Players Group**

Aim

To speak for one minute on a given topic.

Play

* One player is chosen as timekeeper and also picks topics for each player to talk about.
* When it is his or her turn to speak, a player is told his or her topic. This may be anything from a serious topic such as "The current political situation" to something frivolous like "Why women wear hats." Players may choose to treat the subject in any manner they please and what they say may be utter nonsense, provided they do not deviate from the topic, hesitate unduly or repeat themselves.
* Other players may challenge the speaker if they feel he or she has broken a rule. If the timekeeper agrees, then the speaker must drop out and the next player is given a new topic.
* The winner is the player who manages to speak for an entire minute. If, however, two or more players achieve this, the others decide which of the speeches was the best, or alternatively further rounds may be played.

ONE ORANGE

Ages 5–10   *Players* **Group**

Play

❀ The players are seated in a circle.

❀ The player chosen to lead off the game turns to the person on his or her left and says, "One orange."

❀ The phrase is repeated by each member of the circle in turn, until it returns to the player to the left of the first person.

❀ This player must now make up another phrase containing two items beginning with the same letter—for example, "Two tigers."

❀ This is now added to the first phrase, and both are repeated by each player in the circle until it is the turn of the last player.

❀ He or she will now choose a third item. After a few rounds, the phrase all the players must repeat may be something like: "One orange, two tigers, three trains, four feathers, five fingers, six sailors, seven sausages . . ."

❀ When a player makes a mistake, he or she must drop out of the game. The winner is the last player remaining.

TABOO

Age 10+   **Players Group**

Aim

Players try to avoid saying a particular letter of the alphabet.

Play

❀ One player is the questioner and chooses which letter is to be "taboo."

❀ He or she then asks each of the players in turn any question he or she likes.

❀ Players must answer with a sensible phrase or sentence that does not contain the forbidden letter—if they do use the taboo letter, they are out.

❀ The last player to stay in the game wins and becomes the next questioner.

Example

F is TABOO

Questioner: "Name a ball game"

Player 1   "Baseball" STAYS IN

Player 2   "Basketball" STAYS IN

Player 3   "Golf" GOES OUT

TELEPHONE

Age 5+   *Players* **Group**

Play

❀ Players sit in a circle on the floor or along the length of a table. Get one of them to think of a sentence. It should not be spoken out loud.

❀ The first player quietly whispers the sentence to the person on his or her left.

❀ That person then whispers the sentence to the next person in the line. The sentence should only be spoken once and never out loud. On and on it goes until the last player.

❀ The last person then announces the sentence in the form that it has arrived at the end of the line. The first person then announces what the original sentence was. It will probably have changed quite a lot from the original version, causing a great deal of merriment.

❀ There are no winners in this game: it is played just for fun.

TONGUE-TWISTERS

Age 10+   **Players** Group

Equipment
A box or hat.

Preparation
The host should prepare at least ten tongue-twisters in advance and place them in a box or hat.

Play
❋ Each player is invited to pick out a tongue-twister from the box or hat. He or she then has to try to say it ten times in succession without stumbling or hesitating.

❋ Anyone who manages to say his or her tongue-twister ten times without faltering is the winner.

It can be fun compiling original tongue-twisters, perhaps based on the names or interests of one's guests.

Examples of tongue-twisters that might be used include:

**Peter Piper picked a peck
of pickled pepper.**

**Betty bit a blue blob of
bitter blubber.**

One white wren went wrong
one day.

Four fraught farmers
plowing furrowed fields.

Forty throstle thrushes flit
through frightful thistles.

Red lorry, yellow lorry.

The Leith police dismisseth us.

The sixth sick sheik's sixth sheep's sick.

I saw sister Susie sewing shirts
for sailors.

TRAVELER'S ALPHABET

Age 10+   **Players Group**

Aim
Players try to think up alliterative sentences.

Play
❀ The first player says, "I am going on a journey to Amsterdam," or any other town or country beginning with A.

❀ The next person then asks, "What will you do there?" The verb, adjective and noun used in the answer must all begin with A; for example, "I shall acquire attractive antiques."

❀ The second player must then give a place name and an answer using the letter B, the third player uses the letter C, and so on, around the players. Any player who cannot respond is eliminated from the game. If the players wish to make the game more taxing, they may have to give an answer that is linked with the place they have chosen. For example, a player might say, "I am going to Greece to guzzle gorgeous grapes." If a player gives an inappropriate answer, he or she may be challenged by another player. If the challenger cannot think of a more fitting sentence, the first player may stay in the game. Should the challenger's sentence be suitably linked, the first player is eliminated.

❀ The last player in the game wins.

WORD ASSOCIATION

Age 10+ **Players** Group

Play

❋ Players stand in a circle.

❋ The first player says the first word that enters his or her head.

❋ The player to the left has to respond immediately with a word that is somehow linked to the first word—for example, cup = tea = bag = paper, etc. A non-player acts as judge. Players hesitating too long before replying are eliminated. A player may be asked to explain the association between words if his or her reply does not seem to be linked to the previous word.

❋ The last player left in the game is the winner.

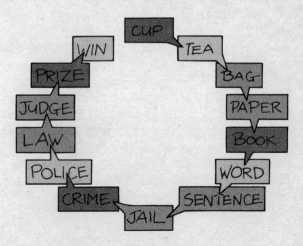

Pen and Paper Games

ACROSTICS

Age 10+   **Players 2**

Aim
Players try to build words out of a given set of letters.

Play

✿ A word of at least three letters is chosen.

✿ Each player writes the word in a column down the left-hand side of a sheet of paper; he or she then writes the same word, but with the letters reversed, down the right-hand side of the page.

✿ The player fills in the space between the two columns with the same number of words as there are letters in the keyword—and starting and ending each word with the letter at either side. For example, if the keyword is "stem," a player's words might read: "scream," "trundle," "earliest" and "manageress."

✿ The winner may be either the first person to fill in all the words, or the player with the longest or most original words.

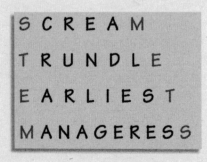

S C R E A M

T R U N D L E

E A R L I E S T

M A N A G E R E S S

ANAGRAMS

Age 10+   **Players** Group

peilmidhun	delphinium
wodronsp	snowdrop
gamirodl	marigold
nedelarv	lavender

Aim

Players try to unscramble jumbled-up words.

Play

❋ One player prepares a list of words belonging to a particular category (e.g., flowers, cities, poets) and jumbles up the letters in each word.

❋ Each of the other players is given a list of the jumbled words and their category and tries to rearrange the letters back into the original words.

❋ The first player to rearrange all the words correctly, or the player with most correct words, after a given time, wins the game.

Variation

More experienced players may like to make up anagrams of their own by rearranging the letters in a word to make one or more other words. For example, "angered" is an anagram of "derange."

BUILD THE TRIANGLE

Age 10+   **Players** Group

Aim
Players try to think of words beginning with a particular letter and of different lengths.

Play
✽ A letter of the alphabet is chosen by the host.
✽ Players are then asked to write it down and build a triangle of words all beginning with the chosen letter, as shown in the example below, adding one letter to each new word. If, for example, the letter chosen is A, the triangle might read as in the illustration below.
✽ The player with the largest triangle wins.

```
                A
              A   S
            A   N   T
          A   L   M   S
        A   D   A   G   E
      A   S   S   E   N   T
    A   V   E   R   A   G   E
  A   D   E   Q   U   A   T   E
```

CATEGORIES

Age **10+**   *Players* **Group**

Aim
Players try to think of words or names within particular categories beginning with particular letters.

Preparation
Each player is given a pencil and a piece of paper. The players decide on between six and a dozen different categories; these may be easy ones for children (e.g., girls' or boys' names, animals, colors) or more difficult for any adults who are also playing (e.g., politicians, rivers, chemicals). Each player lists the categories on his or her other paper. One of the players chooses any letter of the alphabet—preferably an "easy" letter such as "a" or "d" if young children are playing. Older players can make the game more challenging by choosing difficult letters such as "j" or "k." A time limit is agreed.

Play
❋ The players try to find a word beginning with the chosen letter for each of the categories.

❋ They write down their words next to the appropriate category, trying to think of words that none of the other players will have chosen.

❋ When the time is up, each player in turn reads out his or her list of words. If a player has found a word not thought of by any other player, he or she scores two points for that word. If, however, one or more of the other players has also chosen that word, each of them scores one point. If the player could not find a word at all, or if his or her choice of word did not correctly fit the category, he or she gets no points. (Disagreement about the relevance of a word to a category must be resolved by a vote among the other players.)

✱ The winner is the player with the highest score for his or her list of words. Any number of subsequent rounds may be played, using either the same or different categories; the chosen letter, however, must be different for each round. Play-

	Place	Plant	Color
P	Peru	poppy	pink
E	Egypt	endive	ecru
R	Rome	reed	red
S	Seoul	soya	sepia
O	Ohio	orpine	ocher
N	New York	nemesia	navy

ers may take it in turns to choose a letter at the start of a round. Players make a note of their scores at the end of each round. The winner is the player with the highest points total at the end of the final round.

Variation

In a variation, known as Guggenheim, the players choose a keyword of about four to six letters, for example, "person." The letters of the keyword are written spaced out, and players try to find words for each of the categories beginning with each of the letters of the keyword.

Food	Wood	Name
plum	pine	Peter
egg	elm	Edward
ragout	redwood	Robin
soup	sycamore	Sally
orange	oak	Oliver
noodles	nutmeg-tree	Nicola

CROSSWORDS

Age 10+   ***Players*** **Group**

Aim
Players try to make words from letters written in a grid of squares, say five by five.

Play
❀ Each player in turn calls out any letter of the alphabet.

❀ As each letter is called, all players write it into any square of their choice, with the aim of forming words of two or more letters reading either across or down. Generally, abbreviations and proper nouns (names, etc.) may not be used. Once a letter has been written down, it cannot be moved to another square.

❀ Players continue to call out letters until all the individual squares have been filled. The number of points scored is equal to the number of letters in each word (one-letter words do not count). Thus a three-letter word scores three points. If a word fills an entire row or column, one bonus point is scored in addition to the score for that word. No ending of a word can form the beginning of another word in the same row or column. For example, if a row contains the letters "i, f, e, n, d" a player may score four points for the word "fend," but cannot in addition score two points for the word "if."

❀ The winning player is the one with the highest score.

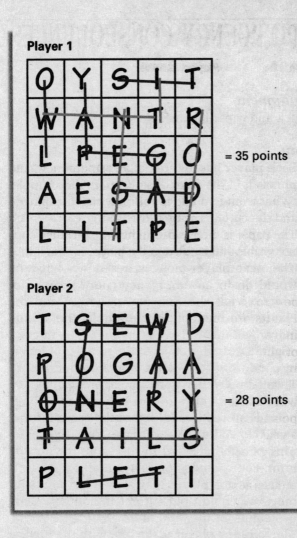

Player 1

O	Y	S	I	T
W	A	N	T	R
L	P	E	G	O
A	E	S	A	D
L	I	T	P	E

= 35 points

Player 2

T	S	E	W	D
P	O	G	A	A
O	N	E	R	Y
T	A	I	L	S
P	L	E	T	I

= 28 points

EMERGENCY CONSEQUENCES

Age 10+   **Players** Group

Equipment
Pencil and paper for each player.

Play
* Each player has to think of an "emergency" and phrase it in the form of a question, for example: "What would you do if your television exploded and the curtains caught fire?"
* The paper is then folded in half so the question is not visible and handed to the player on the left.
* The next player now writes down what he would do in an emergency (not knowing, of course, what the first player wrote) and the results are read out. For example, the second player might respond: "I would boil the kettle and call a vet."
* This game is for amusement only.

What would you do if your father fell down the stairs and broke his leg?

I would set the dog on him and call the police

FAIR AND SQUARE

Age **10+**
Players **Group**

Equipment
Pencil and paper
for each player.

Preparation
Players must draw
a large square on a
piece of paper and
divide it into 25
smaller squares by
drawing four verti-
cal, and four hori-
zontal, lines within
the outline.

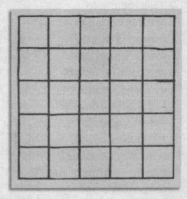

Play
* One player is
  chosen to start
  and calls out a
  letter of the
  alphabet. All the
  players must put
  the letter in one
  of their squares.

* When this is done, the next player chooses a letter and the players decide where to place it in
  their grids. Players may choose the same letter

more than once.

✿ The game continues until all 25 squares are filled. The idea is to arrange your letters so that your grid contains a number of words of three or more letters. Words can run up and down. Players may, of course, choose letters to suit their own needs as their turn arises.

✿ Players score three points for a five-letter word, two points for a four-letter word and one point for each three-letter word.

✿ The winner is the person with the highest score. For example, this player's final score is 19 points, as shown opposite.

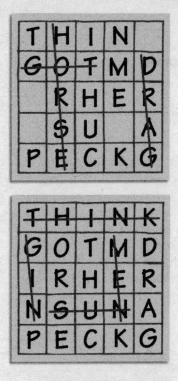

Calculating the score

THINK, HORSE: 3 points each = 6 points.

DRAG, PECK, THIN: 2 points each = 6 points.

INK, GOT, HER, SUN, GIN, MEN, RAG:
1 point each = 7 points.

Total: 19 points.

FILL-INS

Age 10+   **Players** Group

Aim
Players try to guess missing letters in words.

Play
❀ A list of 30–40 words is prepared and kept hidden from the players.

❀ Each player is then given the first and last letters, the number of letters missing, and a clue for each word on the list.

❀ The winner is the first player to fill in all the blanks correctly. Alternatively, the players may be allowed an agreed length of time and then the winner is the player with the most correct words.

E _ _ _ _ R time for eggs (EASTER)

H _ _ _ Y a festive plant (HOLLY)

P _ _ _ _ _ C a peaceful ocean? (PACIFIC)

D _ _ _ _ _ R cleaning cloth (DUSTER)

HANGMAN

Age 10+   **Players 2**

Aim
Players try to guess a secret word.

Play
* One person thinks of a word of about five or six letters.
* This player writes down the same number of dashes as there are letters in his or her word.
* The other players may then start guessing the letters in the word, calling out one letter at a time.
* If the guess is a successful one, the letter is written by the first player above the appropriate dash—if it appears more than once in a word it must be entered as often as it occurs.
* If the guess is an incorrect one, however, the first player may start to draw a hanged man— one line of the drawing representing each wrong letter. The other players must try to guess the secret word before the first player can complete the drawing of the hanged man.
* If one player guesses the word (this should become easier as the game progresses), he or she may take a turn at choosing a word. If the hanged man is completed before the word is guessed, the same player may choose another word. To make the game more difficult, longer words may be chosen. Alternatively, the player

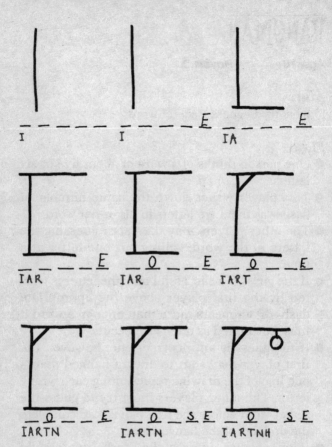

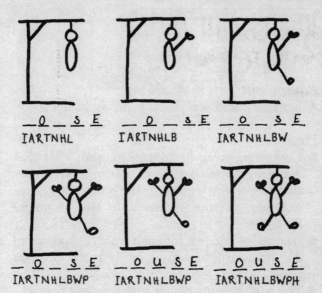

may choose a group of words making a proverb or the title of a book or film and should give the other players a clue as to the category.

✾ In this game the word was "mouse," but the hangman was completed before the word was guessed.

HEADS AND TAILS

Age 10+   *Players* **Group**

Equipment
A dictionary, and pencil and paper for each player.

Play
❀ Players are given 10 minutes to make a list of as
  many words as possible of four or more letters
  that begin and end with the same letter—for
  example, gargling, giving, noun, toot, rectangu-
  lar, bomb.
❀ One point is given for each word, but words of
  six or more letters may be awarded an extra
  point.
❀ The winner is the player with the most points.

Variation

gargling	giving
noun	toot
rectangular	target
suspicious	grabbing
reaper	bomb
delighted	

Older participants could list words that begin and
end with the same two letters—for example—
church, decide, enliven, retire, tomato.

HIDDEN WORDS

Age 10+   **Players Group**

Equipment
Paper and pencil for each player.

Preparation
Make a list of sentences that contain, hidden in consecutive letters, the names of animals or insects—for example: "Thomas wanted to add more sugar to his tea." (Swan, toad) "He knew that it would cost Richard on keyrings alone." (Newt, ostrich, donkey)

Play
✿ Give the players 5 or 10 minutes, depending on the number of sentences, to list all the animals they can find. There may be more than one in each sentence.

✿ The winner will be the player who finds the highest number of animals.

> **Thomas wanted to add more sugar to his tea.**
>
> **Transfer returned money to this slot here.**
>
> **He knew that it would cost Richard on keyrings alone.**

HOW MANY?

Ages 5–10
Players Group

Equipment
Paper and pencil for
each player and some
small household items.

Preparation
Put the household items
in containers. Examples
might include matches,
grains of rice, buttons
and peas. Make a list of
how many of each there
are in each container.

Play
✸ The containers are
   presented, one by
   one, and players
   write down how
   many items they
   think each contains.

✸ Allow players a few
   seconds to look at
   each item and then
   remove it so they
   cannot count the con-
   tents. If there are

more than four competitors, the player whose guess is closest to the correct total scores three points, with the next two closest scoring two and one point, respectively. Bonus points could be awarded for a completely accurate guess.

✿ The player with the highest number of points wins.

JOTTO

Age 10+   **Players Group**

Equipment
Coins, and pencil and paper for each player.

Play
* Players choose a partner. Each pair tosses a coin to see who will start. The first of each pair now writes down a secret five-letter word. None of the letters in that word must be repeated. Examples might include House, Chain, Water.
* The other player now tries to guess the word. He or she also chooses a five-letter word, writes it down and then shows it to the first player.
* The first player looks at the word and writes down next to it which letters in that word are in his or her own hidden word. The letters can be written in any order.
* The second player of each pair now makes another guess and writes it down underneath the first attempt.
* This word is also shown to the first player, who again writes down the letters that are correct.
* The game continues until the second player guesses the first player's word correctly.
* The second player then has a turn at thinking up a five-letter word for the first player to guess.
* The winners are the players in each pair who identify the highest number of secret words in, say, 10 minutes.

Variation

More challenging is for the first player to write only the number of letters in the guessed word which match those in the secret word.

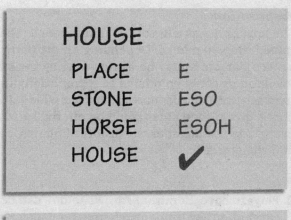

HOUSE

PLACE	E
STONE	ESO
HORSE	ESOH
HOUSE	✔

CHAIN

SPACE	CA
QUACK	CA
CLAIM	CAI
CHAIR	CAIH
CHAIN	✔

NAME THEM!

Age 10+   **Players** Group

Equipment
Paper and pencil for each player.

Preparation
The host prepares a list of 20 famous people, then splits it into 40 names. Depending on the participants, characters may be a wide-ranging general selection or could be related to specific activities such as sports, music, movies, etc. If a wide selection is given, then clues could be offered such as five sports personalities, six historical figures, two film characters, etc.

Play
❀ Players have 10 minutes to write down which surnames they think match up with which first names to create the names of 20 famous people.
❀ The player with the highest number of correct answers is the winner.

1. Cameron   6. Denzel

2. Justin   7. Berry

3. Missy   8. Courtney

4. Brad   9. Britney

5. Bill   10. Jordan

11. Halle

12. Bart

13. Sampras

14. Kobe

15. Gingrich

16. Jones

17. Pitt

18. Mouse

19. Spears

20. Marion

21. Ozzie

22. Powell

23. Pete

24. Aniston

25. Elliott

26. Jennifer

27. Clinton

28. Mickey

29. Colin

30. Nelson

31. Timberlake

32. Washington

33. Osbourne

34. Michael

35. Newt

36. Byrant

37. Mandela

38. Cox

39. Diaz

40. Simpson

ODD MAN OUT

Age **10+**   *Players* **Group**

Equipment
Paper and pencil for each player.

Preparation
The host prepares a number of lists, each containing one item that does not fit in with the others. Below are examples of lists with the "odd man out" in italics:

Play
❋ Players are given a copy of the list and 10 minutes or so to write down which items are the "odd man out."

❋ The player with the highest number of correct answers is the winner.

Hudson, Ohio, *Windermere*, Colorado
(the others are rivers)

Zola, Proust, *Debussy*, Flaubert
(the others were writers)

Bee, scorpion, hornet, *flea*
(the others have stings)

Elizabeth, Victoria, Anne, *Belinda*
(the others were British queens)

New York, Paris, Tokyo, Rome
(the others are capital cities)

Green, yellow, *pink*, blue
(the others are colors of the rainbow)

PHOTOGRAPHIC MEMORY

Age 10+   **Players** Group

Equipment

A postcard or a picture from a magazine, and a piece of paper and a pencil for each player.

Preparation

Ask the guests to look at the picture for 1 minute, after which it is taken away.

Play

❀ The players should be given a piece of paper and a pencil.

❀ They are then asked a number of questions about the picture they have examined, testing their recall of the picture's details. The number and complexity of questions will depend on the age of the players.

❀ The player who answers the most questions correctly is the winner.

RIDDLEMEREE

Age 10+   **Players Group**

Equipment
Paper and pencil for each player.

Play
✿ This involves players choosing a word—an item in the room or a place name—and writing a "riddlemeree," or riddle, giving clues to the letters in the word. Allow players about 10 minutes. The following is an example:

My first is in apple but not in orange,
My second is in kitten but not in cat,
My third is in tea but not in coffee,
My fourth is in green but not in red,
My fifth is in potato and also in carrot.
Answer: "Piano."

✿ Winners are any players who write a riddle that is not solved and any player who works one out.

C	My first is in castle and also in cottage
A	My second is in barter but not in borrow
K	My third is in stake but not in stage
E	My fourth is in tree but not in twig

SCAFFOLD

Age 10+   *Players* **Group**

Equipment
A dictionary, and paper and pencil for each player.

Play
❀ Players are given three letters (at least one of which should be a vowel), and 10 minutes to write down words that contain all three letters. Words must be of four letters or more. Plurals are not allowed.

For example, if the letters are A, M, T, the list of words may include: TEAM, MATE, MEAT, MATADOR, TRAMP, TOMATO, MATCH, ATTEMPT, MATTER . . .

❀ The player with the highest number of correct words will be the winner.

paste   poster   sprite   step

speed   spider   escape   response

separate   **EPS**   precious

persistence   pest   spice

spare   whisper

trespasser   desperation   sleep

SPELLING BEE

Age 7+   **Players Group**

Aim

To spell as many words as possible correctly, so gaining the maximum number of points.

Preparation

One person is chosen as leader, and the other players sit facing him or her. The leader may be given a previously prepared list of words or may make one up. It is a good idea to have a dictionary on hand in case of disputes.

Play

❊ The leader then reads out the first word on the list and the first player tries to spell it.

❊ The player is allowed 10 seconds in which to make an attempt at the correct spelling. If he or she succeeds, one point is scored and the next word is read out for the next player. If the player makes a mistake, the leader reads out the correct spelling. The player does not score for that word, and the next word is read out for the next player. (Alternatively, the player is eliminated from the game for an incorrect answer.) Play continues around the group of players until all the words on the list have been spelled.

❊ The winner is the player with the most points at the end of the game.

BACKWARD SPELLING BEE

Age 7+   *Players* **Group**

In Backward Spelling Bee, a more difficult version
of the game, players must spell their words backward. Scoring is the same as in the standard game.

Variation

For Right or Wrong Spelling Bee, the players should
form two teams, and line up opposite each other.

Play

❋ The leader calls out a word to each player in
turn, alternating between teams.

❋ Each time a player spells a word, the player standing opposite him must call out "Right" or "Wrong."

❋ If he calls a correctly spelled word wrong or a
misspelled word right, he is eliminated from the
game and must leave the line. (Players may
move around once their numbers have been
depleted, so that there is a caller for each player
in the other team.)

❋ If the caller makes a correct call, he gets the
next word to spell.

❋ The last team to retain any players wins.

Street	TEERTS	✔
London	NODNOL	✔
Forward	DARWROF	✘

SURPRISE SENTENCES

Age 7+   *Players* **Teams**

Aim
Each team tries to write a sentence, with each player in the team writing one word of it.

Preparation
For each team, a large sheet of paper is attached to a wall or to a board propped upright.

Play
❋ Each team lines up opposite its sheet of paper and the leader is given a pencil.

❋ At the word "Go!" the leader runs up to his or her team's paper and writes any word he or she likes and then runs back to the team, hands the pencil to the next player and goes to the end of the team.

❋ As soon as the next player gets the pencil, he or she goes to the paper and adds a second word either in front of, or behind, the leader's word.

❋ Play continues in this way with each player adding one word. The words should be chosen and put together so that they can be part of a grammatically correct sentence.

❋ Each player, except the last, must avoid completing the sentence. The last player should be able to complete the sentence by adding just one word and he or she also puts in the punctuation.

❀ Players may not confer and choose a sentence before writing their words.

❀ The first team to construct a sentence with one word from each player wins the game.

SWARMING ANTS

Age 10+
Players Group

Equipment
Pencil and paper
for each player.

Preparation
On a piece of
paper, write down
the phrases listed
on the right: ("A
shining ant," "A
floating ant," etc.).

Play
❋ The players
   have to write
   down a word
   ending in -ant
   that relates to
   the clue. Some
   examples are
   shown.
❋ The player with
   the highest
   number of cor-
   rect answers is
   the winner.

A shining ant
   brilliant

A floating ant
   buoyant

A sweet-smelling ant
   fragrant

A green ant
   verdant

A singing ant
   chant

A plentiful ant
   abundant

A waiting ant
   attendant

A non-stop ant
   constant

A sloping ant
   slant

A graceful ant
   elegant

A telltale ant
   informant

TANGLED SENTENCES

Ages 5–10   **Players Group**

Aim

To scramble up sentences in a way that makes it hard to guess what they are meant to be.

Play

❀ Players write down a sentence, which might be a popular saying, a line from a pop song or poem, or a newspaper headline. However, instead of writing it down properly, they write it with the words scrambled in such a way as to make a strange or funny sentence, such as "Make never wrongs a two right" from "Two wrongs never make a right." The sentences being scrambled might be quite simple, if the players are young, or quite complicated for older children.

❀ Really, this is a game played just for the fun of it, but the winner might be the player whose tangled sentence is the most difficult to unscramble.

chickens hatch before your count don't they
(DON'T COUNT YOUR CHICKENS BEFORE THEY HATCH)

feather a flock of birds together
(BIRDS OF A FEATHER FLOCK TOGETHER)

a wall sat Humpty on Dumpty
(HUMPTY DUMPTY SAT ON A WALL)

TELEGRAMS

Age 10+   **Players** Group

Aim

Players make up a message from a list of letters or a given word.

Play

❋ Players are given or make up a list of 15 letters and must use each of them—in the order given—as the initial letter of a word in a 15-word telegram. (Alternatively, the players are given or select a word of about 10–15 letters, e.g., blackberries—the first word must begin with "b," the second with "l," and so on.) The telegram may include one or two place names and may—if the player wishes—have the name of the "sender" as the last word. Stops (or periods) may be used for punctuation.

❋ The winner is the first player to complete his or her telegram, or, if a time limit has been set, the player whose telegram is judged to be the best at the end of the time set.

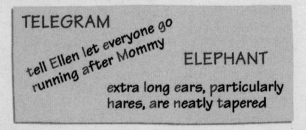

TELEGRAM

tell Ellen let everyone go running after Mommy

ELEPHANT

extra long ears, particularly hares, are neatly tapered

TRANSFORMATION

Age 10+   **Players Group**

Aim
Players try to "transform" one word into another through a series of intermediate stages.

Play
❋ Two words with the same number of letters are chosen.

❋ Each player writes down the two words.

❋ He or she then tries to change the first word into the second word by altering only one letter at a time and each time forming a new word. For example, "dog" could be changed to "cat" in four words as below.

❋ It is easiest to begin with three- or four-letter words until the players are quite practiced—when five- or even six-letter words may be tried.

❋ The winner is the player who completes the changes using the fewest number of words.

DOG

DOT

COT

CAT

WHAT'S NEXT?

Age 10+   **Players** Group

Equipment
Paper and pencil for each player.

Preparation
The host prepares a number of "progressions" in advance. These can be numerical or alphabetical. Examples are:

What is the next number in this sequence? 5 6 8 11... (Answer: 15).

What is the next letter in this sequence? A E I M... (Answer: Q).

In the first example, you add one to five to make six, then add two to six to make eight, and add three to eight to make eleven. To continue the sequence, therefore, you must add four to eleven to make fifteen. Likewise, in the second example, there are three letters missing between each entry in the sequence.

Play
✿ The players are allowed 3 minutes or so to work out what letter or number comes next in each progression.

✿ The winner is the player with the most correct answers.

Answers to sequences at right are:
128; IR; 28; T; 32; J; 85; 34; 4,294,967,296.

1 2 4 8 16 32 64 ....

MN LO KP JQ ....

1 2 3 4 6 9 13 19 ....

Z B X D V F ....

31 28 31 30 31 ....

J F M A M J ....

5 9 13 21 33 53 ....

1 1 2 3 5 8 13 21 ....

2 4 16 256 65,536 ....

WHO IS IT?

Age 10+
Players Group

Equipment

Paper and pencil for each player, a good pile of photographs of famous people cut out from newspapers and magazines, and some card.

Preparation

The host should have cut out part of each photograph so that it shows the eyes only. Each should then be stuck onto the card. Each picture should now be labeled with a number or letter, and a note, kept by the organizer, of the celebrity whose eyes feature in each picture. Each player should also get a list of the celebrities.

Playing

* The "eyes" are passed around the table, and everyone has to write down the name of the personality to whom they belong.
* The winner is the participant making the most correct guesses.

WORD SQUARE

Age 10+   **Players Group**

Equipment
Pencil and paper for each player.

Preparation
Write, in large capital letters and, as shown below, the words "WORLD" and "EARTH" on each piece of paper, and give one to every player. Other combinations can be used, but make sure both words are of the same length so that the Word Square can be completed.

Playing
❈ The players have to think of words comprising five letters that can fit in between, as in the example below.
❈ The first player creating a Word Square is the winner.

W	r	i	t	E
O	p	e	r	A
R	o	v	e	R
L	i	g	h	T
D	i	t	c	H

WORD-MAKING

Age 10+   **Players** Group

Equipment
A dictionary, and pencil and paper for each player.

Preparation
Think of a long word and give each player a pencil and a sheet of paper.

Playing
✿ Players are given a long word, which they write down on the top of their sheet of paper.
✿ They have 10 minutes to make as many new words of at least three letters from the word they have been given. For example, if they are given HELICOPTER, they might make a list containing: TOP, CLIP, TRIPE, HOTEL, REPEL, CHOIR and POLICE.
✿ The player who writes down the most new words (no plurals or proper names are allowed) will be the winner. Five- or six-letter words may count double.

PHOTOGRAPHY

ANDREW	LEANNE
rat	graph
hot	hot
pat	got
pay	pot
tray	pay
harp	trap
part	tray
root	rot
hoop	gap
troop	party
graph	pray
rap	goat
hat	happy
hog	

INDEX

ESSENTIAL REFERENCE TOOLS
FROM HARPERTORCH

RTHE CONCISE
Roget's
INTERNATIONAL
THESAURUS®
REVISED & UPDATED
SIXTH EDITION

**The world's number-one bestselling
thesaurus of synonyms, antonyms,
and related words**

Edited by Barbara Ann Kipfer, Ph.D.
Robert L. Chapman, Ph.D., Consulting Editor

0-06-009479-6/$5.99 US/$7.99 Can

HARPER
COLLINS

NEWLY REVISED AND UPDATED

WEBSTER'S
DICTIONARY

**A new, up-to-date, completely portable
version of America's most
well-known dictionary**

0-06-055782-6/$5.99 US/$7.99 Can